Non-Verbal Reasoning

The 11+
Study Book
and Parents' Guide

For GL & other test providers

This book contains two pull-out sections:

A **Benchmark Test** at the front
A **Parents' Guide to 11+ Non-Verbal Reasoning** at the back

Practise • Prepare • Pass

Everything your child needs for 11+ success

11+ Non-Verbal Reasoning — Benchmark Test

There are 36 questions in this test and it should take about 20 minutes. Find the answer to each question and write its letter on the line. If you get stuck on a question, move on to the next one.

Section One

Find the figure in each row that is **most unlike** the other figures.

1.

      a   b   c   d   e   (___)

2.

      a   b   c   d   e   (___)

3.

      a   b   c   d   e   (___)

4.

      a   b   c   d   e   (___)

Find which one of the five squares **completes the sequence** on the left.

5.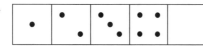

               a   b   c   d   e   (___)

6.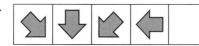

               a   b   c   d   e   (___)

7.

               a   b   c   d   e   (___)

8.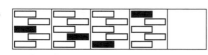

               a   b   c   d   e   (___)

Find the figure on the right which is **most like** the two figures on the left.

9.

               a   b   c   d   e   (___)

10.

                a   b   c   d   e   (___)

11.

                a   b   c   d   e   (___)

12.

                a   b   c   d   e   (___)

/12

NHRE1

CGP

Non-Verbal Reasoning

The 11+ Study Book
and Parents' Guide

For GL & other test providers

Practise • Prepare • Pass
Everything your child needs for 11+ success

CONTENTS

Question Types

Similarities and Differences

Pairs, Series and Grids

Codes

Published by CGP

Editors:
Anthony Muller, Rebecca Tate, Luke von Kotze

With thanks to Claire Boulter and Judy Hornigold for the proofreading.

ISBN: 978 1 84762 831 2

Printed by Elanders Ltd, Newcastle upon Tyne
Clipart from Corel®

Based on the classic CGP style created by Richard Parsons.

What's in the 11+

Make sure you've got your head around the basics of the 11+ before you begin.

The **11+** is an **Admissions Test**

1) The 11+ is a test used by <u>some schools</u> to help with their <u>selection process</u>.

2) You'll usually take it when you're in <u>Year 6</u>, at some point during the <u>autumn term</u>.

3) Schools <u>use the results</u> to decide who to accept. They might also use <u>other things</u> to help make up their mind, like information about <u>where you live</u>.

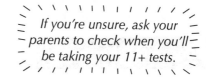

If you're unsure, ask your parents to check when you'll be taking your 11+ tests.

Some Schools test a **Mixture** of **Subjects**

1) Depending on the <u>school</u>, the 11+ can be a test on <u>different subjects</u>.

2) There are <u>four</u> main subjects that can be tested in the 11+, so you might sit papers on <u>some</u> or <u>all</u> of these:

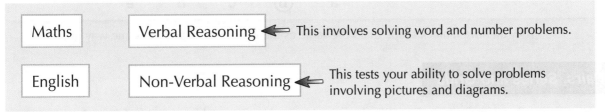

| Maths | Verbal Reasoning | ← This involves solving word and number problems. |
| English | Non-Verbal Reasoning | ← This tests your ability to solve problems involving pictures and diagrams. |

3) This book will help you with the <u>Non-Verbal Reasoning</u> part of the test.

Get to **Know** what **Kind** of **Paper** you're taking

Your paper will either be <u>multiple choice</u> or <u>standard answer</u>.

Multiple Choice

1) For each question you'll be given some <u>options</u> on a <u>separate answer sheet</u>.

2) You'll need to mark your answer with a <u>clear pencil line</u> in the box next to the <u>option</u> that you think is <u>correct</u>.

Look out for the 'Tips and Tricks' boxes in this Study Book — they'll give you practical advice about the test.

Standard Answer

1) You'll be expected to <u>write down</u> or <u>circle</u> the correct letter.

2) You'll still have the same <u>five letters</u> to choose from, though.

Check which type of <u>question paper</u> you'll be taking, so you know what it <u>looks</u> like and <u>where</u> your answers go. Try to do some practice tests in the <u>same format</u> as the test you'll be taking, so you know what to <u>expect</u> on the day.

What's in the 11+ Non-Verbal Reasoning Test

Get your brain ready for Non-Verbal Reasoning by reading about the different question types.

Non-Verbal Reasoning *involves* Solving Problems

1) Non-Verbal Reasoning is about shapes and patterns.
2) Although you won't have learnt how to answer Non-Verbal Reasoning questions at school, you've probably already picked up some of the skills you need for the test.
3) There are a few different question types that can crop up. We've grouped them into categories:

Similarities and Differences

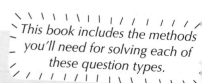

This book includes the methods you'll need for solving each of these question types.

You'll need to spot similarities and differences between different figures to answer these questions. Here's an example:

Q Find the figure that is most like the two figures on the left. Circle its letter.

They all have a black shape that's the same as the white shape, and the same way up.

Pairs, Series and Grids

You'll need to work out what fills the gap in a series, a grid or a pair of figures. Here's an example:

Q Find the figure that is the missing square from the series. Circle its letter.

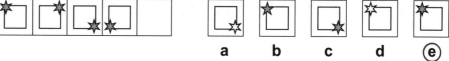

There's a grey, six-pointed star moving clockwise round the corners of the square.

Codes

You'll need to work out the code for a figure by looking at the codes you're given for some other figures. Here's an example:

Q On the left are figures with code letters that describe them. Work out what the code letters mean and then find the code for the shape on the right from the five options.

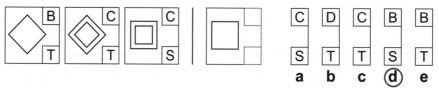

B means there's only one shape, S means it's got a flat side at the bottom.

How to Prepare for the 11+

Give yourself a head start with your Non-Verbal Reasoning preparation — be organised and plan ahead.

Divide your Preparation into Stages

1) You should find a way to prepare for the 11+ that <u>suits you</u>. This may depend on <u>how much time</u> you have before the test. Here's a good way to <u>plan</u> your Non-Verbal Reasoning practice:

> | Do the Benchmark Test at the front of this book. Ask an adult to mark it for you. |
> | :-: |
> | ↓ |
> | Learn strategies for answering different question types using this Study Book. |
> | ↓ |
> | Do plenty of practice questions, concentrating on the question types you find tricky. |
> | ↓ |
> | Sit some practice papers to prepare you for the real test. |

2) When you <u>first</u> start answering Non-Verbal Reasoning questions, try to solve the questions without <u>making any mistakes</u>, rather than working <u>quickly</u>.

3) Once you feel <u>confident</u> about the questions, then you can build up your <u>speed</u>.

4) You can do this by asking an adult to <u>time</u> you as you answer a <u>set of questions</u>, or by seeing <u>how many</u> questions you can answer in a certain <u>amount of time</u>, e.g. 5 minutes. You can then try to <u>beat</u> your time or score.

5) As you get closer to the test day, work on getting a <u>balance</u> between <u>speed</u> and <u>accuracy</u> — that's what you're <u>aiming for</u> when you sit the real test.

There are Many Ways to Practise the Skills you Need

The <u>best way</u> to tackle Non-Verbal Reasoning is to do lots of <u>practice</u>. This isn't the only thing that will help though — there are other ways you can <u>build up the skills</u> you need for the test:

1) Try drawing different <u>shapes</u> on a piece of paper. Use a <u>small mirror</u> to investigate what they look like when they've been <u>reflected</u>.

2) Copy shapes onto <u>tracing paper</u> to look at how different shapes <u>change</u> when you <u>rotate</u> them. This will help you to <u>spot changes quickly</u>.

3) Do activities like <u>jigsaw puzzles</u>, <u>origami</u>, <u>tangrams</u> (see p.15), <u>draughts</u>, <u>sudoku</u> and wooden or metal <u>puzzles</u> to help you to develop your <u>problem solving skills</u>.

4) Try the <u>warm-up</u> activities on the pages about each question type in this Study Book. They'll introduce you to the kinds of <u>skills</u> you'll use to answer each type of question.

Spotting Patterns

In this section you'll be able to try your hand at all the different parts of Non-Verbal Reasoning. You need to get the hang of everything that can happen in a question if you want to do well.

What you might **Have** to **Do**

1) The best way to get good at Non-Verbal Reasoning is to do lots of questions, but first you need to know what you're looking out for. This section will help you get used to spotting the main elements of questions before you get into the details of how each question type works.

2) The real 11+ test will have questions which mix different things together. They won't be split up like they are in this section, but learning about them separately will help you understand how the real questions work.

If you can't solve a questio[n] look at the answer (but n[ot] the explanation) and try t[o] work out why it's the righ[t] one. If you're still stuck, look at the explanation.

3) If you get stuck when working through some real 11+ style questions, you can look back at this section to help you understand what's going on.

Questions are made up of **Different Parts**

This section is a good place to start if you're new to Non-Verbal Reasoning or if you want extra practice, because it deals with all the things you'll come across in full 11+ questions.

Even if you're confident about an element, you can use the practice questions for some extra practice.

Learn about and practise **Each** of the **Elements Separately**

1) Shapes — the different shapes, the importance of different numbers of sides, and symmetry.

2) Counting — when to count, what to count, and how to use basic maths.

3) Pointing — how arrows can point in directions, as well as at, or away from, an object.

4) Shading and Line Type — the different line types and shadings that a shape can have.

5) Position — where a shape is positioned in a figure.

6) Order — what an order is and how it works if the objects in an order move or change.

7) Rotation — how much an object is turned (its angle) and in what direction.

8) Reflection — when a mirror image of a shape is made by reflecting it across a mirror line.

9) Layering — how and in what ways shapes can overlap.

Some equipment will **Help** you **Understand** the **Different Elements**

1) As you're going through this book, you may find it helpful to have a pen, pencil and some scrap paper. Doing a rough drawing of how you think a figure should look in questions that you're struggling with might help you work out the answer.

2) A protractor might help you see the angle and direction a figure is turned. If you have an analogue clock or watch, this might also help with clockwise and anticlockwise directions.

3) A mirror will help you understand reflection and symmetry.

4) Once you've got to grips with the basics in this book, you should put everything away apart from a pen, pencil and rough paper, as you won't be able to use the other things in the real test.

Shapes

Shapes are everywhere in Non-Verbal Reasoning. To do well, you'll need to get really good at spotting the similarities and differences between them.

Warm-Up Activity

Cut a square, a triangle and a circle out of a piece of scrap paper. See how many <u>different ways</u> you can <u>fold</u> each one in <u>half</u> so both sides are exactly the <u>same</u>.

Shapes have different **Numbers** of **Sides**

You can tell what <u>type of shape</u> something is by how <u>many sides</u> it has, so you should always count the <u>number</u> of sides of different <u>shapes</u> in a question.

Shapes of the **Same Type** can **Look Different**

1) Even though the shapes below have the same number of sides, they look <u>different</u>. That's because their <u>sides</u> are different <u>lengths</u> or their <u>angles</u> are different.

These shapes are all triangles...

... and these are all rectangles.

2) Some shapes will look really <u>different</u>, but they might still have the <u>same</u> number of sides.

These are all quadrilaterals — they have four sides.

These are all hexagons — they have six sides.

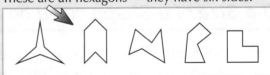

You'll need to **Count** the **Sides** of different shapes

Lots of questions use <u>sequences</u> based on the <u>number of sides</u> that shapes have.

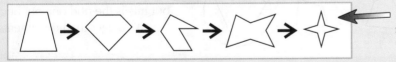

In this example, the number of sides goes up by one each time — four, five, six, seven and eight.

Some shapes have **Curved Sides**

Don't forget to count <u>curved sides</u> as well.

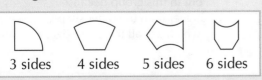

3 sides   4 sides   5 sides   6 sides

Look out for questions where you only need to look at the number of curved sides. In this example, the five-sided shape is different to the others because it's the only one with two curved sides.

The **Sides** of a **Shape** could be **Important**

For some questions you will have to spot which shapes are <u>similar</u> and which are <u>different</u>.

Shapes might be different because they have **Different Numbers** of **Sides**

Sometimes you'll need to spot a shape that has a different <u>number of sides</u> from the rest. This can be <u>tricky</u> if all the shapes look very <u>different</u>.

The fourth shape is the odd one out because it has four sides, not three.

Shapes might be different because they have **Different Lengths** of **Sides**

You might have to spot <u>one different</u> shape in a group that all have the <u>same</u> <u>number</u> of sides. Look for shapes with different <u>angles</u> or sides of different <u>lengths</u>.

These shapes are all triangles, but the third one is different. Its sides are different lengths — the other triangles all have three sides of equal length.

The **Size** of a **Shape** could be **Important**

You can compare the <u>size</u> of <u>any shapes</u>, even if they're <u>completely different</u>.
Look for shapes that are <u>obviously bigger</u> or <u>smaller</u> than the rest.

1) A <u>shape</u> might be a <u>different size</u> to other shapes, even though it has the same number of sides. This can be quite easy to spot if the other <u>shapes</u> are all the <u>same</u>.

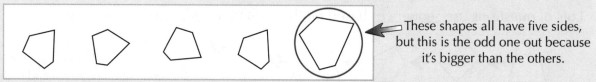

These shapes all have five sides, but this is the odd one out because it's bigger than the others.

2) <u>Different shapes</u> might be the <u>same size</u>, even if they have <u>different numbers of sides</u>. When the numbers of sides are all different, they <u>won't help you</u> spot the odd one out — you'll need to look for <u>another difference</u>.

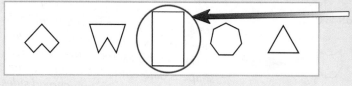

The rectangle is the odd one out in this group because it's bigger than the other shapes, which are all the same size.

Some shapes are **Symmetrical**

A shape is <u>symmetrical</u> if you can <u>draw</u> a <u>line</u> through it that <u>divides</u> the shape into <u>halves</u> which are <u>mirror images</u> of each other.

1) Imagine that the shape is <u>folded in half</u> along a line that goes through the middle of the shape. If the two sides fit together <u>exactly</u>, the shape is symmetrical.

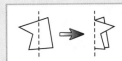 These shapes are both symmetrical. If they're folded along the dotted line the sides match up exactly.

2) If the two halves aren't <u>exactly</u> the same, the shape <u>isn't symmetrical</u>.

 No matter where you fold this shape, the two halves don't match up.

You'll often have to think about **More Than One** shape

1) Sometimes the <u>type of shape</u> won't be important — you'll need to look at other things like <u>shading</u>, or whether its <u>outline</u> is solid, dotted or dashed (see p.12-14).

2) For a lot of questions, you'll have to think about <u>other things</u>, such as — Do the shapes have <u>different rotations</u>? What is their <u>total number</u> of <u>sides</u>? How are they <u>positioned</u> in <u>relation</u> to <u>other objects</u>?

Practice Questions

1) Which shape is the odd one out? Circle the right letter.

If any of these questions don't make sense, check out the different question types on p.30, p.33 and p.40.

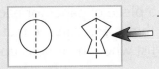

  a   b   c   d   e

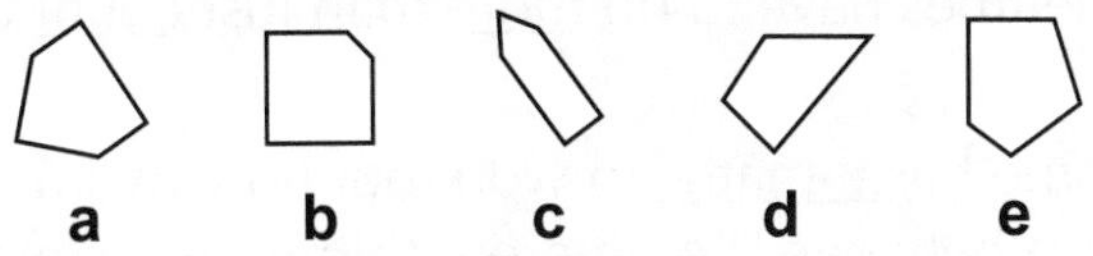

2) Which shape is the most like the first two shapes? Circle the right letter.

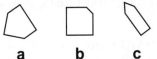   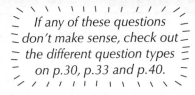

  a   b   c   d   e

3) Which shape comes next in the series? Circle the right letter.

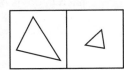   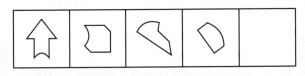

  a   b   c   d   e

Counting

If in doubt, count everything — shapes, sides, dots and lines. The solution to a tricky-looking question could be as simple as how many of something there are.

Warm-Up Activity

Find another person to play this game with you. Get a pen and a piece of paper for each of you. Set a timer for two minutes, and then make a list of all the things you can see that are circles, e.g. a coin or the top of a cup. See who has the longest list when the time is up.

You'll **Often** need to **Count Things**

In easier questions it might be as simple as counting to five.

1) For some figures it will be obvious what you should count.

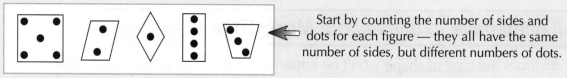

Start by counting the number of sides and dots for each figure — they all have the same number of sides, but different numbers of dots.

2) For others it will be less obvious what you should count.

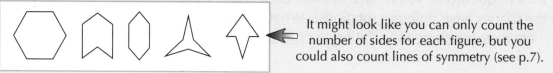

It might look like you can only count the number of sides for each figure, but you could also count lines of symmetry (see p.7).

You might have to **Add** or **Subtract**

If there is more than one type of object, you sometimes have to do more than just count each one.

1) For harder questions you'll need to do some basic maths to work out how two numbers relate to each other. Look for relationships between the different things you can count.

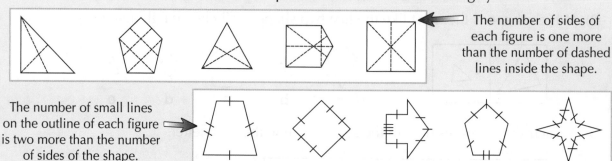

The number of sides of each figure is one more than the number of dashed lines inside the shape.

The number of small lines on the outline of each figure is two more than the number of sides of the shape.

2) Keep track of all the numbers of different elements in each figure. You'll find the answer to some questions by noticing that there is a pattern in the difference between two of these numbers, or in their total when added together.

Spotting Patterns

Equal Numbers of Different Objects could be Important

Add different elements together to see if their total is equal to the number of another element.

If you're looking for connections between figures, try every counting combination.

For these figures, you could count grey shapes, black shapes, circles, squares, sides and lines (among other things).

In all these figures the number of lines added to the number of grey shapes is the same as the number of sides of the large shape.

You won't just have to spot when different figures have the same number of objects. You'll also have to notice when different figures all have an odd or even number of objects.

Counting is Important in Series Questions

You will often have to add or subtract for series questions.

See p.40 for more on Series Questions.

Counting will tell you how many of each thing are added or subtracted, so you can work out what should come next.

7 points, 1 dot   6 points, 2 dots   5 points, 3 dots   4 points, 4 dots

The star is losing a point in each figure, but gaining a dot. The next figure will have three points and five dots.

Practice Questions

1) Which figure is the odd one out? Circle the right letter.

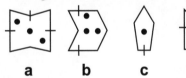

    a   b   c   d   e

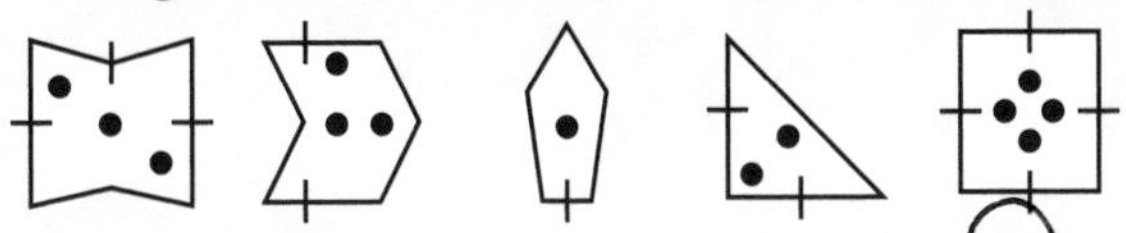

2) Which figure is the most like the first two figures? Circle the right letter.

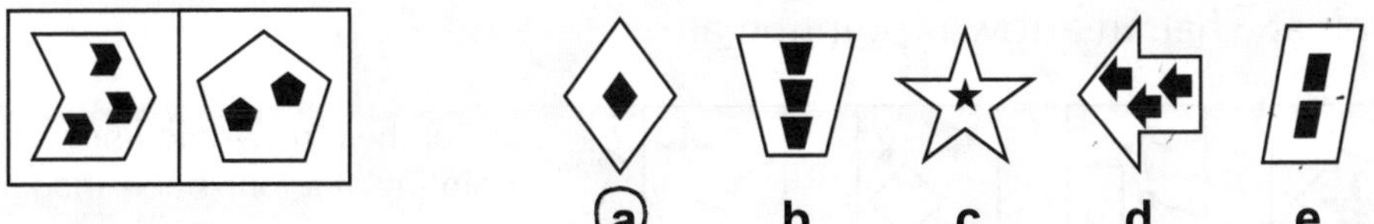

                      a   b   c   d   e

3) Which figure comes next in the series? Circle the right letter.

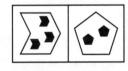   

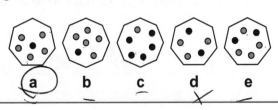

                                a   b   c   d   e

Pointing

Don't just look at what arrows are pointing at — it might also be important what an arrow is pointing away from, or what direction it's pointing in.

Warm-Up Activity

Cut a <u>circle</u> and an <u>arrow</u> out of card. Using a pen, divide the circle into <u>six equal sections</u>, and <u>number them</u> from <u>one</u> to <u>six</u>. Make a hole in the middle of the circle and the arrow, then use a split pin to attach them together. Try using your <u>spinner</u> instead of a dice in a board game.

Arrows Point in a Direction

Arrows can point <u>up</u>, <u>down</u>, <u>left</u> and <u>right</u>, as well as <u>diagonally</u>, so you need to look at the exact direction an arrow is <u>pointing</u>.

1) It helps to know the <u>different directions</u> that an arrow can <u>point</u>.

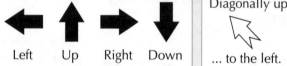

Left   Up   Right   Down

Diagonally up...
... to the left.   ... to the right.

Diagonally down...
... to the left.   ... to the right.

2) You need to notice when arrows point in the <u>same direction</u> or a <u>different direction</u>.

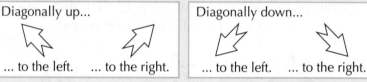

There is only one arrow that points in a different direction from the others.

An arrow-style line is a line with a small shape at one end instead of an arrowhead.

You should treat arrow-style lines like these as normal arrows.

Arrows can Point At Objects

As well as <u>direction</u>, you should also check if an arrow is <u>pointing towards</u> or <u>away from</u> something

1) You need to look at <u>what</u> an arrow is <u>pointing at</u>.

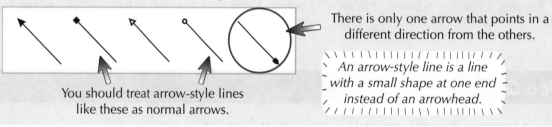

All of the arrow-style lines are pointing at a four-sided shape.

2) It may also be important to look at what an arrow is <u>pointing away from</u>.

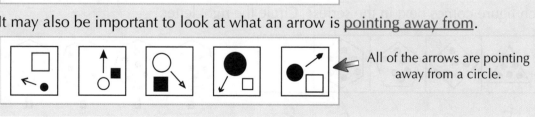

All of the arrows are pointing away from a circle.

Arrows *can point* Clockwise *or* Anticlockwise

Not all arrows just <u>point</u> in a <u>straight line</u>, some arrows also <u>go</u> in a <u>circular direction</u>.

1) <u>Clockwise</u> means the <u>direction</u> in which the <u>hands</u> on a <u>clock move</u>. <u>Anticlockwise</u> means the <u>opposite direction</u>.

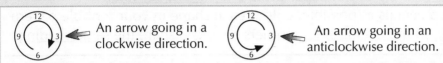

An arrow going in a clockwise direction.

An arrow going in an anticlockwise direction.

2) All these arrows point in a <u>clockwise direction</u>.

Both straight arrows with corners and curved arrows can point in a clockwise or anticlockwise direction.

3) All these arrows point in an <u>anticlockwise direction</u>.

It might help you work out if an arrow is going clockwise or anticlockwise if you imagine it going round an invisible clock face.

4) Arrows <u>next to shapes</u> can also suggest a <u>clockwise</u> or <u>anticlockwise direction</u>.

The figures with anticlockwise arrows are circled in red.

Practice Questions

1) Which figure is the odd one out? Circle the right letter.

  a   **b**   **c**   **d**   **e**

2) Which arrow comes next in the series? Circle the right letter.

  a   **b**   **c**   **d**   **e**

3) Which arrow is the most like the first two arrows? Circle the right letter.

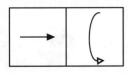 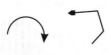   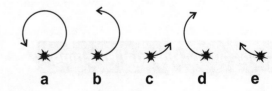

  a   **b**   **c**   **d**   **e**

Spotting Patterns

Shading and Line Types

Every shape that you come across will be drawn with a particular type of line, and shaded in a particular way. Recognising different line types and shadings will be an important skill for the test.

Warm-Up Activity

It's possible to colour in scribble patterns like this using only four colours.

Draw a <u>scribble pattern</u> on a piece of paper using <u>one continuous line</u>. Using as <u>few</u> coloured pencils as possible, colour each shape in your scribble pattern so that <u>no two shapes</u> with <u>touching sides</u> (corners are okay) share the <u>same shading</u>.

Shapes can be Shaded in Different Ways

There are other weird shadings that sometimes appear. If you come across any, don't be put off — treat them like any other type of shading.

There are a few <u>main ways</u> that shapes are shaded.

Look out for the <u>most common types</u>:

| White | Black | Grey | Hatched | Spotted |

There are Different Types of Hatching

Hatching is when shapes are shaded with lines.

It's not always enough to <u>notice</u> that a shape is <u>hatched</u>, you also need to look at <u>how</u> it is hatched.

Check the Direction of the Hatching

It's easy to miss <u>different types</u> of hatching unless you <u>check</u> each hatched shape <u>carefully</u>.

These shapes are all hatched in different directions.

 Vertical hatching   Horizontal hatching   Hatching going diagonally down to the left.   Hatching going diagonally down to the right.

Look out for Unusual Hatching

You could even get a question where the number of hatched lines is important.

You might get a shape that is <u>hatched</u> in an <u>unusual way</u> — just treat it like <u>any other</u> hatched shape.

These shapes are also hatched, but with different types of hatching. ⇨ 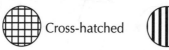 Cross-hatched   Thick hatching   White hatching on a black shape

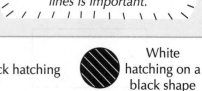

Spotting Patterns

Different Shapes might share the Same Shading

When there are <u>lots</u> of <u>shaded shapes</u>, you could look for shapes that are shaded the <u>same</u>.

1) If the answer to a question is about the <u>shading</u> of <u>large shapes</u> it might be <u>obvious</u>.

In this Odd One Out, it's obvious that the third shape is shaded differently from the rest.

2) If the answer to a question focuses on the <u>shading</u> of <u>more than one shape</u>, or a <u>smaller part</u> of a figure, it might be <u>trickier</u> to spot.

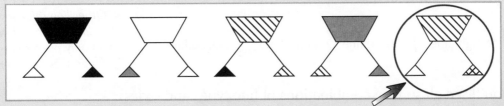

This Odd One Out is quite tricky, but by checking all the shapes and comparing them, you can work out the answer. The fifth figure is the only one with a small right hand shape shaded differently from the large shape.

The Amount a Shape is Shaded could be Important

<u>Different parts</u> of shapes can be shaded, but the <u>total amount</u> of shading might be the <u>same</u>. You might need to <u>work out</u> what <u>fraction</u> of a shape is <u>shaded</u>.

1) Sometimes you will need to use <u>basic maths</u> to work out <u>how much</u> is <u>shaded</u>.

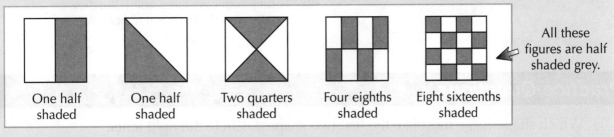

| One half shaded | One half shaded | Two quarters shaded | Four eighths shaded | Eight sixteenths shaded |

All these figures are half shaded grey.

2) You might have to <u>add</u> two <u>different amounts</u> of shading <u>together</u>.

The shading of these two figures added together equals one whole shape.

The shading of these two figures added together equals three quarters of a whole shape.

3) You might have to work out <u>how much</u> shading needs to be <u>added</u> or <u>taken away</u> from a figure.

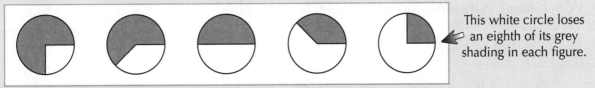

This white circle loses an eighth of its grey shading in each figure.

Spotting Patterns

Lines can be *Drawn Differently*

The lines of <u>figures</u>, <u>arrows</u> and the <u>outlines</u> on shapes can be <u>different line types</u> and <u>styles</u>. You don't need to <u>remember</u> them, but you need to be able to <u>spot</u> which lines are <u>different</u> in a question.

Check for *Different Line Types* and *Styles*

1) These are the most common <u>line types</u>.

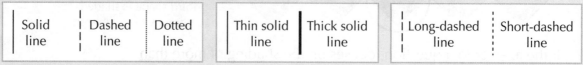

| Solid line | Dashed line | Dotted line | | Thin solid line | Thick solid line | | Long-dashed line | Short-dashed line |

2) Lines also come in <u>different styles</u>.

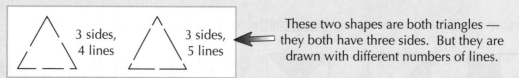

| Straight line | Curved line | Wavy line | Jagged line |

Other line thicknesses and lengths of line dashes might come up, but you only need to be able to spot the differences between different lines.

3) You'll see <u>all sorts</u> of combinations of <u>line types</u> and <u>styles</u>.

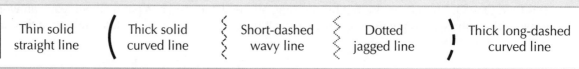

| Thin solid straight line | Thick solid curved line | Short-dashed wavy line | Dotted jagged line | Thick long-dashed curved line |

Watch out for shapes with *Different Lengths* of *Dashes* in their *Outline*

The <u>number of lines</u> used to <u>draw</u> a shape isn't always the <u>same</u> as its <u>number of sides</u>.

3 sides, 4 lines   3 sides, 5 lines

These two shapes are both triangles — they both have three sides. But they are drawn with different numbers of lines.

Practice Questions

1) Which shape is the most like the first two shapes? Circle the right letter.

a   b   c   d   (e)

2) Which figure comes next in the series? Circle the right letter.

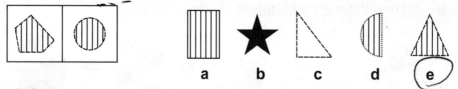

a   b   c   (d)   e

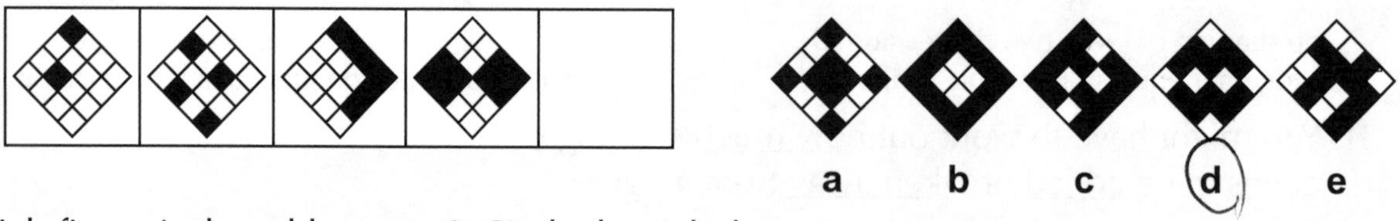

3) Which figure is the odd one out? Circle the right letter.

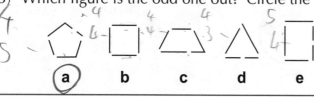

(a)   b   c   d   e

Position

Position is all about where something is — whether an object is at the top, the bottom, the left or the right of a figure — and it could be important in working out the answer to a question.

Warm-Up Activity

Trace over the shapes on the right and draw them on a new piece of paper. Position the shapes together to make different shapes. Can you use all of the shapes and make them into one complete square?

This is called a tangram.

Every Object has a Position

Noticing <u>where</u> something is sounds <u>simple</u>, but it's easy to <u>miss something obvious</u>.

Objects can have <u>similar</u> or <u>different positions</u>. <u>Keeping track</u> of <u>each shape's position</u> helps you <u>spot similarities</u> and <u>differences</u>.

Taken together, the position of both the rectangle and the star is not the same in any of these figures, but in all of the figures the rectangle is always at the top, and the star is always on the left.

Objects also have a Position in Relation to Other Objects

When there's <u>more</u> than <u>one shape</u>, each object has a <u>position</u> other than just its <u>own</u>.

1) Two <u>objects</u> may be in <u>different positions</u> in different figures, but in the same position in <u>relation</u> to <u>each other</u>.

The trapezium and the spot are in different positions in each figure, but the spot is directly above the trapezium in all the figures.

2) In harder questions where there are <u>more than two</u> objects, you will need to look at the position of <u>each object</u> in relation to <u>all</u> the <u>other objects</u>.

In this Odd One Out, the circle is to the left of the cross in every figure except for the fifth one. The square's position doesn't matter.

Objects can **Move Position** in a **Sequence**

You might have to work out <u>how</u> an object is moving so you can decide <u>where</u> it should be <u>next</u>. Some object movements are <u>more common</u> than others.

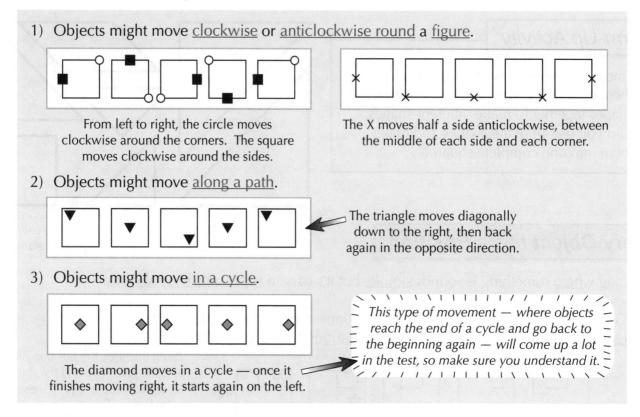

1) Objects might move <u>clockwise</u> or <u>anticlockwise round</u> a <u>figure</u>.

From left to right, the circle moves clockwise around the corners. The square moves clockwise around the sides.

The X moves half a side anticlockwise, between the middle of each side and each corner.

2) Objects might move <u>along a path</u>.

The triangle moves diagonally down to the right, then back again in the opposite direction.

3) Objects might move <u>in a cycle</u>.

This type of movement — where objects reach the end of a cycle and go back to the beginning again — will come up a lot in the test, so make sure you understand it.

The diamond moves in a cycle — once it finishes moving right, it starts again on the left.

The **Position** of **New Objects** is **Important**

When an object is <u>added</u> to a figure you need to look at <u>where</u> the <u>new object</u> is <u>positioned</u>.

1) Once you've worked out <u>what</u> is being <u>added</u>, you need to work out <u>where</u> it is added.

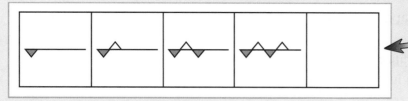

In this Series question, grey triangles and white triangles are added in turn. The missing square must have an extra grey triangle, and it must be below the line on the right hand side of the figure.

All of these figures have the right number of triangles in the right colours, but only the second figure has the grey triangle in the correct position.

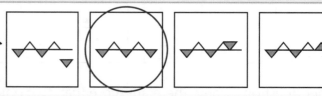

2) In some questions, <u>two or more</u> figures are <u>added together</u> to make a <u>third figure</u>.

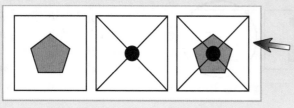

The first figure is added to the second figure to make the third figure. The position of both figures inside the square stays the same. The second figure goes in front of the first figure.

The **Position** of objects that are **Removed** can be **Important**

It's not enough to notice when something is <u>removed</u> — you need to notice <u>where</u> it's <u>removed from</u>.

1) Objects or parts of an object can be <u>removed</u> in <u>different ways</u> and <u>from different positions</u>.

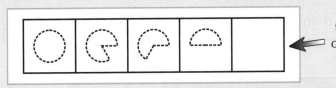

In this Series question the circle loses a sixth each time, so the next square must have a circle fraction of two sixths. The circle always loses the sixth going in a clockwise direction, so the next sixth must be removed from the left hand side of the semicircle.

All these figures have the correct circle fraction, but only the fourth figure has it in the correct position

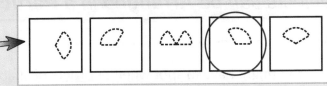

2) Even if <u>two figures</u> are <u>not the same</u>, you can see what objects should be <u>removed</u> by looking at their <u>positions</u>.

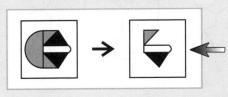

For both of these pairs, to get from the first figure to the second remove the top black shape, the bottom grey shape and the left hand shape.

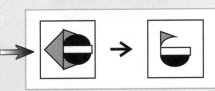

Practice Questions

1) Which figure comes next in the series? Circle the right letter.

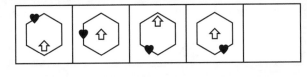

   a   **b**   **c**   **d**   **e**

2) Which figure is the odd one out? Circle the right letter.

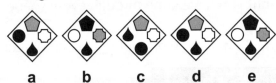

  a   **b**   **c**   **d**   **e**

3) Which figure comes next in the series? Circle the right letter.

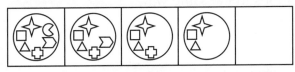

   a   **b**   **c**   **d**   **e**

Order

When you arrange two or more objects into a group or line, you've put them in an order.

Warm-Up Activity

Find <u>three different coins</u> and see how many <u>different orders</u> you can <u>line them up</u> in.

Objects can be **Arranged** in a **Particular Order**

Any <u>group</u> of shapes in a <u>line</u> can be seen as having an <u>order</u>.

You might have to spot whether <u>orders of shapes</u> are the <u>same</u> or <u>different</u>.

All these figures are in the same order except for the circled figure, where the circle and the hexagon have swapped places.

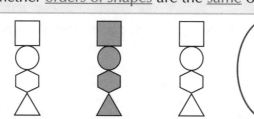

Some orders are the **Same** but **Look Different**

Shapes don't have to be in the <u>same positions</u> to be in the <u>same order</u>.

Choose a **Starting Point** to **Check** an order

1) You can check if an order is the <u>same</u> by <u>starting</u> with the <u>same object</u> and then <u>counting</u> the rest of the objects <u>in turn</u>.

All these figures go from left to right in the order: triangle, diamond, pentagon, except for the circled figure.

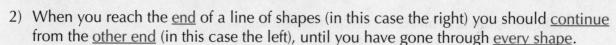

2) When you reach the <u>end</u> of a line of shapes (in this case the right) you should <u>continue</u> from the <u>other end</u> (in this case the left), until you have gone through <u>every shape</u>.

Objects can <u>move</u> but keep the <u>same order</u>. You might have to work out <u>how</u> each object is <u>moving</u>.

If an **Order Moves** Check **What Happens** to the **End Object**

If all the objects in a line of shapes <u>move positions</u> in the same way, the <u>end object</u> moves to the <u>beginning</u> of the order.

All of these shapes have moved one place to the right. When a shape cannot move any further right, it appears again on the left.

The movement just means the order <u>starts</u> with a <u>different shape</u>. If the objects <u>moved another place</u> to the <u>right</u> they'd be arranged: X shape, heart, circle, triangle (from left to right).

Objects can be **Ordered Around** a **Shape**

Objects round a shape might have a <u>clockwise</u> or an <u>anticlockwise arrangement</u>.

1) Pick a <u>starting point</u> and <u>work round</u> the shape in the <u>same direction</u> to <u>check the order</u>.

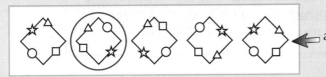

In this Odd One Out the shapes in the second figure are arranged in a different order from the rest. It goes circle, star, square, triangle in a clockwise direction. (The rest go circle, star, triangle, square.)

2) Different figures can have the <u>same circular order</u> but they might <u>look different</u>.

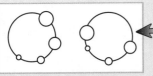

These two figures have the same order. The circles are in size order, from biggest to smallest, going in a clockwise direction.

This figure looks similar, but it's arranged in size order, from biggest to smallest, going in an anticlockwise direction.

There might be **More Than One Order** in a question

If there is <u>more than one order</u>, and each order <u>moves about</u>, it can be <u>hard to spot</u> what's going on.

1) <u>Shading</u> is often used as a <u>separate order</u>, for example:

The order stays the same for both shading and shapes, but the orders have moved.

2) To work out how the <u>two orders move</u> you can <u>separate them</u>.

All the shapes move one place to the left. It goes from triangle, square, circle to square, circle, triangle.

All the shadings move one place to the right. It goes from black, cross-hatched, hatched to hatched, black, cross-hatched.

Practice Questions

1) Which figure is the odd one out? Circle the right letter.

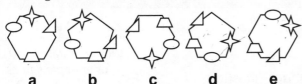

    a   **b**   **c**   **d**   **e**

2) Which figure comes next in the series? Circle the right letter.

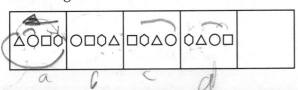   

    a   **b**   **c**   **d**   **e**

Rotation

Rotation is when an object is turned, either around its own centre, or around another point.

Warm-Up Activity

Draw a picture on a piece of paper. Without turning the page, try drawing how you think the picture would look upside down on a separate piece of paper. Turn the original piece of paper round to see how close you got.

Rotation is when a Shape is Turned

An object can be turned in different ways, and it will often look different after it has been rotated.

Different rotations of a shape look different from each other.

This is the same shape rotated six times. Each figure looks different because it's rotated a different amount (or angle).

Shapes can rotate Different Amounts and in Different Directions

Objects can rotate in a clockwise or anticlockwise direction.

There are lots of Different Angles

See p.11 for more on clockwise and anticlockwise directions.

1) You'll need to recognise these angles of rotation, and work out the correct direction.

 45°   90°   180°

 Clockwise   Anticlockwise

2) Knowing about angles will help you work out how much a shape is rotated.

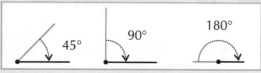 45°   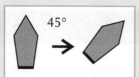 90°   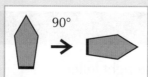 180°

The shape is rotated clockwise in each example.

Series Questions often use Rotation

Some shapes look the same when they are rotated 180 degrees — for example figures 1 and 5.

This shows how shapes might rotate in a series question.

This figure is rotated 90 degrees clockwise each time.

This figure is rotating 45 degrees anticlockwise each time.

Rotation **Disguises** whether shapes are the **Same** or **Different**

Rotation can make shapes <u>look different</u>, even when they are the <u>same</u>.

It can be <u>even harder</u> to see whether a <u>complicated shape</u> has been rotated.

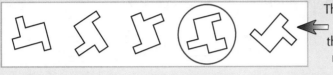

The rotation makes it hard to spot that the fourth shape is different. Picking a point that looks the same in each shape and following the edge might help you see if each shape is the same.

Only the fifth figure is the same as the first two — but the rotation makes all the figures look similar.

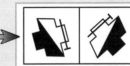  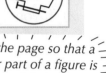

Turning the page so that a particular part of a figure is at the top might help you recognise similar shapes.

Parts of a figure might **Rotate** on their **Own**

The <u>different parts</u> of a figure don't have to <u>rotate together</u> — a <u>part</u> might rotate <u>on its own</u>, or in a <u>different way</u> to the <u>rest of the figure</u>.

1) In a <u>complicated figure</u>, only a <u>small part</u> might <u>rotate</u> (often other things will be happening).

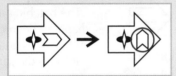

Only the small white arrowhead is rotated — the rest of the figure stays the same.

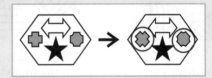

Only the small grey shapes are rotated — the rest of the figure stays the same.

2) Sometimes <u>part</u> of a figure will <u>rotate round another part</u> of the figure.

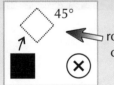

This square rotates 45 degrees clockwise round the circle.

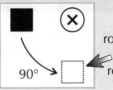

This square rotates 90 degrees anticlockwise round the circle.

This square rotates 180 degrees round the circle — it could be in either direction.

Different Objects might **Rotate Differently**

In harder questions, you need to check the rotation of <u>each object separately</u>.

If you <u>assume</u> that everything is <u>rotating</u> in the <u>same way</u> you could make a <u>mistake</u>.

The black shape rotates 45 degrees anticlockwise each time.

 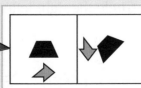 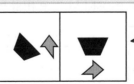

The grey shape rotates 90 degrees clockwise around the black shape.

Hatched Shapes have Complicated rotations

Because <u>hatching</u> is made up of <u>angled lines</u> it can also be <u>rotated</u>.

1) You should check <u>hatched shading carefully</u>, because it might not <u>rotate</u> in the <u>same way</u> as the shape.

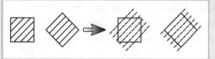   

The square rotates, but the hatching stays the same.

The hatching rotates, but the square stays the same.

2) If you think the <u>shape</u> and the <u>hatching</u> are rotating <u>differently</u>, you should <u>always</u> <u>double check</u>. Work out the <u>shape's rotation first</u>, then look at the <u>hatching</u>.

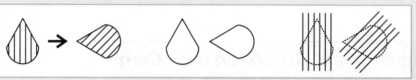

There are two rotations here.

The shape rotates 90 degrees anticlockwise.

The hatching rotates 45 degrees clockwise.

3) <u>Hatching</u> looks the <u>same</u> rotated <u>90 degrees clockwise</u> or <u>90 degrees anticlockwise</u>.

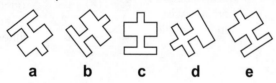

Original shapes

90° clockwise rotations

90° anticlockwise rotations

The hatching rotates with the shape 90 degrees clockwise and 90 degrees anticlockwise, but it looks the same both ways.

Practice Questions

1) Which shape is the odd one out? Circle the right letter.

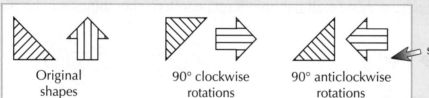

a   b   c   d   e

2) Which figure comes next in the series? Circle the right letter.

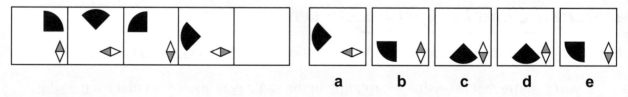

a   b   c   d   e

3) Which figure is the most like the first two figures? Circle the right letter.

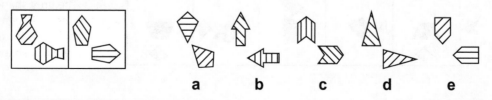

a   b   c   d   e

Reflection

If you look in a mirror you will see your reflection. Reflecting a shape or an object is the same idea, except that you're doing it on a piece of paper instead of in a mirror.

Warm-Up Activity

Draw a <u>picture</u> on a piece of paper. Then, try to draw how the picture would look if you held it up to a <u>mirror</u>. Use a real mirror to check how <u>close</u> your drawing was to the <u>reflection</u>.

Reflection is when a shape gets **Flipped** across a **Mirror Line**

A <u>reflected shape</u> should look like the <u>original shape</u> as if it was seen in a <u>mirror</u>.

Reflections use a **Mirror Line**

1) If you were to put a <u>real mirror</u> along a <u>mirror line</u> you would see in the mirror <u>how</u> the original shape should be <u>reflected</u>.

2) The shapes on <u>either side</u> of the mirror line should be <u>identical</u> to <u>each other</u>, except that one has been <u>flipped over</u>.

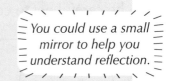
You could use a small mirror to help you understand reflection.

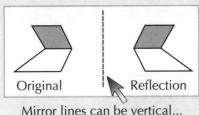

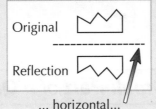

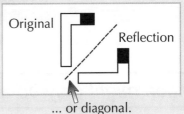

Mirror lines can be vertical...
(Shape is reflected across)

... horizontal...
(Shape is reflected downwards)

... or diagonal.
(Shape is reflected diagonally)

Most **Reflection Questions Won't** show you a **Mirror Line**

<u>Spotting</u> that a shape is <u>reflected</u> is half the battle, so it helps to get used to <u>recognising reflections</u>. Think about how shapes would <u>look</u> if they were reflected.

If you work out where the <u>mirror line should go</u> it will help you see whether one shape is a <u>reflection</u> of another.

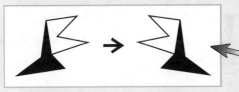

It's obvious that the right hand figure is a reflection of the left hand shape.

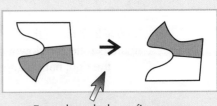

Even though these figures are next to each other, the right hand shape is a downwards reflection of the left hand shape.

Even though these figures are next to each other, the right hand shape is a diagonal reflection of the left hand shape.

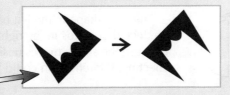

A reflection won't always tell you <u>where</u> the shape should be, only what it should <u>look like</u>.

Spotting Patterns

With **Some Shapes** it's **Hard** to **Spot** a **Reflection**

Even simple reflections can be a bit <u>tricky</u> — especially if a <u>hatched shape</u> is involved.

1) Some reflected shapes look the same as the <u>original shape</u>.

This figure has been reflected across the mirror line, but it looks the same on both sides of the dashed line.

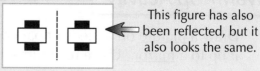

This figure has also been reflected, but it also looks the same.

2) <u>Hatched shapes</u> might give you a <u>clue</u> as to whether a <u>shape</u> has been reflected, because <u>hatching</u> can also be <u>reflected</u>.

Shapes that look the same after a reflection must always have at least one line of symmetry.

Diagonal hatching looks like it's been rotated 90 degrees if it's reflected across or downwards. If it's reflected diagonally, it will look the same as it does on the original shape.

3) <u>Parallelograms</u> only look <u>slightly different</u> if they are reflected — you should be careful not to confuse a <u>reflected</u> parallelogram with a <u>rotated one</u>.

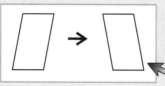

This figure shows how a parallelogram is reflected — it would look the same if it was reflected downwards or across.

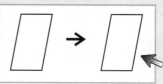

A 180 degree rotation of a parallelogram looks the same as it does before it's rotated.

Reflection might only be a **Small Part** of a **Question**

In <u>complicated questions</u> reflection might only be <u>part</u> of everything that's going on, so you need to <u>check carefully</u> for reflected shapes.

1) In questions where there is a <u>lot happening</u>, it could be <u>easy</u> to <u>miss</u> a <u>reflection</u>.

The bottom shape reflects across in each series square.

2) In some questions you might have to <u>work out</u> how <u>one figure turns into another</u>.

The black shape in the left hand figure is reflected downwards in the right hand figure.

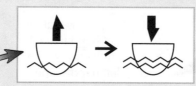

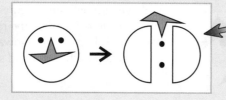

The grey shape in the left hand figure is reflected upwards in the right hand figure. Because the shape moves position as well as reflecting, the reflection could be hard to spot.

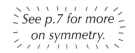

Be **Careful** not to **Confuse Reflection** with **Rotation**

See p.7 for more on symmetry.

<u>Rotation</u> and <u>reflection</u> often <u>appear together</u>, so you need to be able to <u>tell</u> the <u>two apart</u>.

*Check that a **Rotation** isn't **Hiding** a **Reflection***

<u>Unsymmetrical figures</u> which are <u>reflected</u> cannot be <u>rotated</u> to <u>match</u> the <u>original figure</u>.

  90° rotation 270° rotation

No matter how the reflected shape is rotated, it won't look the same as the original.

Original   Reflection   180° rotation

The circled figure is a reflection of all the other shapes, but this is hidden by its rotation. ⇨

*Questions with **Reflected** shapes that **Also Rotate** can be **Tricky***

If a figure <u>rotates</u> and <u>reflects</u> at the <u>same time</u>, it's hard to work out what's <u>happening</u>.

In this sequence the shape rotates 90 degrees anticlockwise each time, then reflects across its longest side. You can tell that it must reflect because no matter how you rotate each shape it won't match the next shape in the sequence.

Practice Questions

1) Which figure is the odd one out? Circle the right letter.

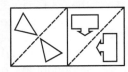   a   b   c   d   e

2) Which figure is the most like the first two figures? Circle the right letter.

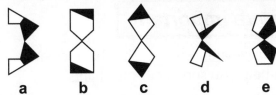

 a   b   c   d   e

3) Which figure comes next in the series? Circle the right letter.

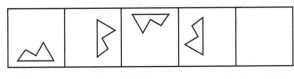

 a   b   c   d   e

Spotting Patterns

Layering

Layering is when a shape is in front of or behind another shape. Imagine putting a book on top of another book. If you looked at the pile of books from the side you would see that it has two layers.

Warm-Up Activity

Find <u>five different objects</u> (e.g. a mug, a ruler), a pencil and a piece of paper. <u>Draw around</u> each of the objects so that their <u>outlines overlap</u>. <u>Colour</u> in the parts of your picture where the <u>shapes overlap</u>.

Shapes can **Overlap** in **Different Ways**

You might see <u>all</u> the <u>outlines</u> of <u>overlapping shapes</u>, or one shape might be <u>in front of</u> the other.

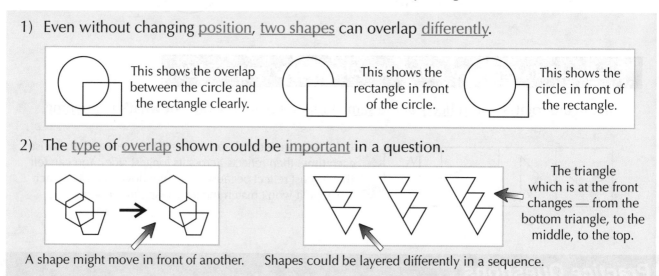

1) Even without changing <u>position</u>, <u>two shapes</u> can overlap <u>differently</u>.

This shows the overlap between the circle and the rectangle clearly.

This shows the rectangle in front of the circle.

This shows the circle in front of the rectangle.

2) The <u>type</u> of <u>overlap</u> shown could be <u>important</u> in a question.

A shape might move in front of another.   Shapes could be layered differently in a sequence.

The triangle which is at the front changes — from the bottom triangle, to the middle, to the top.

The **Shapes Created** by an **Overlap** are **Important**

Try treating the overlap between the two shapes as a <u>separate shape</u>. The shape created by an <u>overlap</u> can look a bit strange, which might help you spot a <u>cut-out shape</u>.

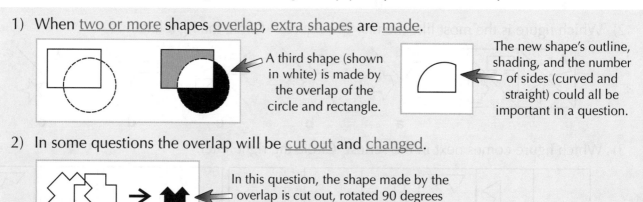

1) When <u>two or more</u> shapes <u>overlap</u>, <u>extra shapes</u> are <u>made</u>.

A third shape (shown in white) is made by the overlap of the circle and rectangle.

The new shape's outline, shading, and the number of sides (curved and straight) could all be important in a question.

2) In some questions the overlap will be <u>cut out</u> and <u>changed</u>.

In this question, the shape made by the overlap is cut out, rotated 90 degrees anticlockwise and turned black.

Spotting Patterns

Shapes can be Ordered by Layer

In questions where shapes <u>overlap</u> it might be important how they are <u>arranged</u>
— you should check which shape is at the <u>front</u> and which is at the <u>back</u>.

1) If there are <u>lots</u> of figures that are <u>layered</u>, you could look at what <u>all</u> the shapes
   at the <u>front</u> or <u>back</u> have in <u>common</u>.

The black shape is at the front of each figure, and the white shape is always at the back.

2) Where <u>two shapes overlap</u> in each figure, the shapes at the <u>front</u> might all
   be different, but be <u>related</u> to the shapes <u>behind</u> them in the <u>same way</u>.

The shape with the most sides is always at the back — the shape with the fewest sides is always at the front.

*Some questions will have **More Than One Overlap***

In questions with <u>lots of overlapping</u> shapes you need to look at <u>more</u> than just
the <u>front</u> and <u>back shapes</u> — you also need to look at <u>all</u> the shapes <u>in between</u>.

Look at how **Shapes** are **Layered** on top of **Each Other**

Overlapping shapes can be <u>positioned</u> in <u>different ways</u>.

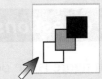

These three shapes can be layered in the same order but in different positions.

Going diagonally up to the left. From front to back — black, grey, white.

Going diagonally down to the left. From front to back — black, grey, white.

Look at how **Every Shape** is **Layered** in a figure

1) Figures can also be layered so that <u>every shape</u> overlaps <u>each other</u>.

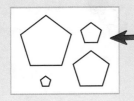

These shapes are all identical, apart from their size.

These are the same shapes layered directly in front of each other.

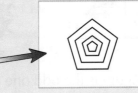

2) Watch out for figures where <u>every shape</u> is <u>layered</u>, but not every shape <u>overlaps</u>.

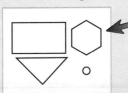

These shapes are all different.

These are the same shapes layered in front of each other. Even though they don't all overlap you can still see the order the shapes are layered in.

Layered *shapes might* Change Position, Layer *or* Colour

If layered shapes <u>change colour</u> or <u>position</u>, you should <u>double check</u> whether the <u>order</u> of the shapes <u>stays the same</u> or not.

1) Sometimes <u>layered shapes</u> will <u>change</u> without moving.

These shapes stay in the same position, but the shading moves back (or out) one shape each time.

2) Sometimes layered shapes will <u>move positions</u> or <u>layers</u>.

These circles move positions but stay in the same layers.

These circles stay in the same positions but change layers.

3) Because layered shapes are <u>ordered</u> from <u>front to back</u> they can also <u>move layers</u> and still be in the <u>same order</u>.

See p.18-19 for more about order.

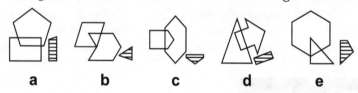

Although all of these figures move positions and layers, they still have the same order — C shape, rectangle, arrow-style line, triangle — they just have different shapes at the front.

Practice Questions

1) Which figure is the odd one out? Circle the right letter.

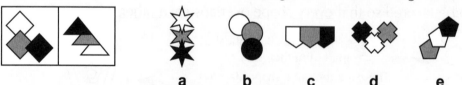

    a   **b**   **c**   **d**   **e**

2) Which figure is the most like the first two figures? Circle the right letter.

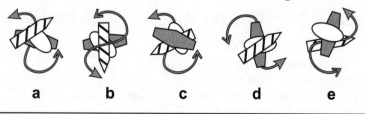

        a   **b**   **c**   **d**   **e**

3) Which figure is the odd one out? Circle the right letter.

        a   **b**   **c**   **d**   **e**

Similarities and Differences

The questions on this page are all about finding a figure that's the same as or different from another group of figures. They're a bit like spot the difference puzzles... only different.

*You'll need to **Compare** different figures*

1) These questions are all about spotting <u>similarities</u> and <u>differences</u> between figures.

2) To find the right answer, you'll have to <u>compare</u> the different <u>elements</u> of the figures, like shading or shape. Look back at pages 4-28 to <u>remind</u> yourself what to look for.

3) There are <u>two</u> types of question in this section:

Odd One Out

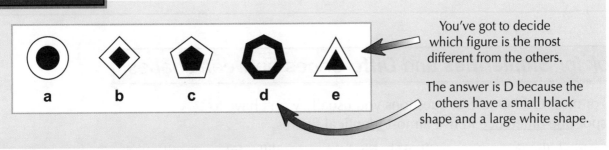

You've got to decide which figure is the most different from the others.

The answer is D because the others have a small black shape and a large white shape.

Find the Figure Like the Others

1) Here's a <u>Find the Figure Like the Others</u> question:

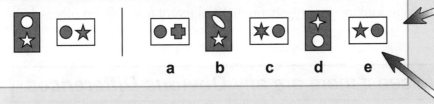

You've got to decide which of the figures on the right is the most similar to the two figures on the left.

The answer is E. Every figure must have a circle and a five-pointed star.

2) <u>Find the Figure Like the Others</u> questions can have <u>two</u> figures on the left hand side, or they can have <u>three</u> figures. You can work out the answer for both in <u>exactly the same way</u>.

Writing Notes can help you learn how to do these questions

Here are some <u>useful tips</u> for <u>starting out</u> with these questions.

1) As you go through the <u>different parts</u> of each question to decide which ones will help you find the answer, <u>write down</u> the ones you've already looked at. This will stop you from looking at the same one <u>twice</u>. If you're <u>stuck</u> on a question, look back at the list of elements on page 4 and see if you're <u>missing</u> any from your list.

2) If you're <u>counting</u> something in each figure (e.g. the number of dots or the number of sides), <u>write down</u> how many you count for each one to help you <u>keep track</u> of the numbers.

These tips are useful when you're <u>learning</u> how to do the questions, but as you get <u>closer</u> to the <u>test</u>, you'll need to learn to keep track of these things <u>in your head</u>.

Odd One Out

For these questions, all you've got to do is spot the odd one out. Sounds pretty easy, but sometimes the pesky thing's hidden really well... Here are some tips to help you hunt it down.

Warm-Up Activity

1. Find another person to play this game with you. Each draw <u>five boxes</u> on a piece of paper and draw a <u>picture</u> inside <u>each box</u>. The pictures should all <u>look different</u>, but <u>four</u> should have something in <u>common</u> that the other one <u>doesn't</u> (e.g. four different cars and one lorry).

2. <u>Cut out</u> the boxes, <u>shuffle</u> them and <u>swap</u> them with the other person.

3. <u>Time</u> how long it takes each of you to find the picture that's <u>different</u> from the other four and say <u>why</u> it's the <u>odd one out</u>. The person who does this the <u>fastest wins</u>.

Look for **Similarities** and **Differences** between shapes

1) For most Odd One Out questions you usually won't have to spot <u>one difference</u> in five almost <u>identical</u> figures.

2) Instead, the five options will probably look quite <u>different</u> — you'll need to spot what <u>four</u> of them have <u>in common</u>, and <u>one</u> of them doesn't.

Tips and Tricks for Odd One Out questions

Watch out for questions where two out of five figures have something in common — remember that you're looking for <u>one</u> shape that's different from <u>all</u> the others.

Look at the figures to see if there are any **Obvious Differences**

Sometimes the answer to an Odd One Out question will be <u>quite simple</u>.

> **Q** Find the figure that is most unlike the other four figures. Circle its letter.
>
>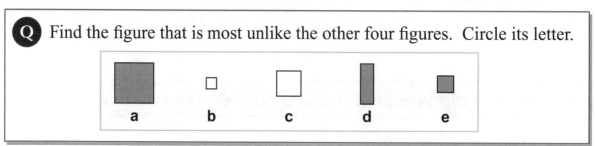
>
>   **a**   **b**   **c**   **d**   **e**

⌐ Method 1 — Look for a simple answer

See if you can spot anything <u>straight away</u> — then quickly <u>check</u> your answer.

1) In this example, the odd one out must be <u>D</u> (a rectangle) because all the other figures are <u>squares</u>.

2) Look at the other elements to make sure you're right. All the shapes are <u>different sizes</u>, so you can't use size to spot the odd one out. Two figures are <u>white</u> and three are <u>grey</u> — this means that shading <u>isn't relevant</u>.

Question Types — Similarities and Differences

If the answer isn't *Obvious*, go through each *Element* one by one

Sometimes you won't be able to spot the odd one out straight away.

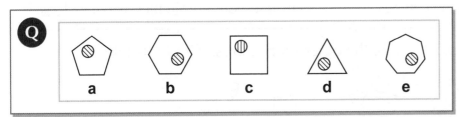

Method 2 — Look at each element in turn

1) Think about the different elements that can come up (see p.4).

2) Check each one in turn until you find something that four figures share, and one doesn't.

1) Large shapes — they're all different, and there's nothing that four out of five have in common.

2) Small shapes — they're all circles that are the same size.

3) Position — the circles are in different positions in each white shape — position doesn't help you find the odd one out.

Don't spend too long on this method. If you're stuck, go on to the method below.

4) Shading — the large shapes are all shaded the same. All the small circles are hatched, but only four have the same direction of hatching. C has vertical hatching — the others all have hatching going diagonally down to the right, so the answer is C.

Sometimes you'll have to think about *More Than One Element*

In some questions you can only spot the odd one out by looking at a combination of different elements.

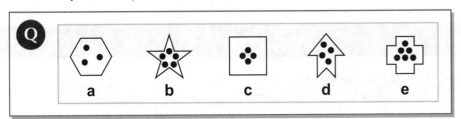

In this example, you could look at the number of sides the shapes have, the number of dots, the size of the shapes and the symmetry of the shapes without finding the answer. You need to try the next method:

Method 3 — Look at more than one element at a time

Look at how the elements work together — try to find links between them.

1) Count the sides of the white shapes — A has 6, B has 10, C has 4, D has 8, and E has 12. They all have different numbers of sides and they are all even, so you need to look at something else.

2) Count the number of black dots — A has 3, B has 5, C has 4, D has 4, and E has 6. You need to find something that four figures have in common, so this doesn't help either.

3) Compare these numbers — A has 6 sides and 3 dots, B has 10 sides and 5 dots, C has 4 sides and 4 dots, D has 8 sides and 4 dots, and E has 12 sides and 6 dots.

4) This shows that the white shapes in A, B, D and E have twice the number of sides as the number of black dots. C has the same number of sides as black dots, so it's the odd one out.

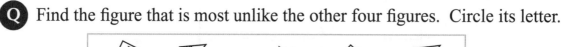

Sometimes the answer is *Simpler* than it *Looks*

If you can't find the answer after looking at all the elements in each figure and at different combination of elements, try looking at the simple things again — some questions are simpler than they look.

Q Find the figure that is most unlike the other four figures. Circle its letter.

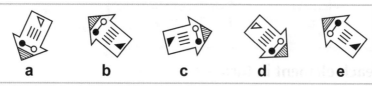

Go through the elements again, to see if you've missed anything:

1) Shading — two arrows have a different direction of hatching at the tip.

2) Number of lines — two figures have five lines and three figures have four lines.

3) Shading of triangle — two figures have white triangles and three have black triangles.

4) Rotation of triangle — all of the triangles rotate with the arrow. None of them are reflected.

5) Shading of circles — every figure has one black circle and one white circle.

6) Position of circles — in A, C, D and E, the black circle is on the right of the shape when the arrow is pointing up. In B it's on the left of the shape. This means that B must be the odd one out.

Tips and Tricks for Odd One Out questions

When the figures all look similar but are rotated differently, it might help to turn the page so you can look at them all the same way up.

Practice Questions

Which figure is the odd one out? Circle the right letter.

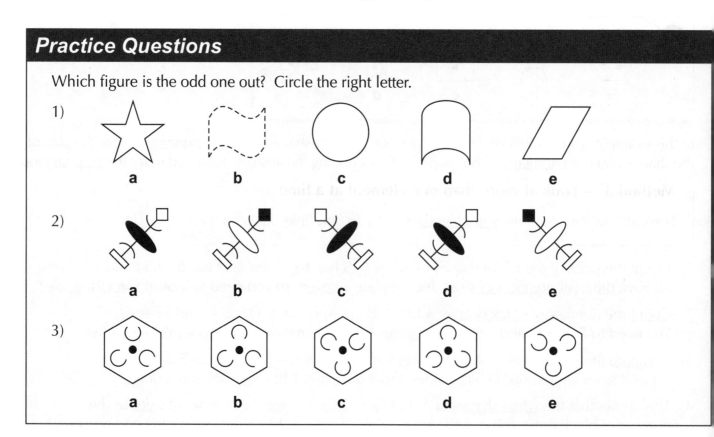

Question Types — Similarities and Differences

Find the Figure Like the Others

These questions are a bit like Odd One Out questions — you'll still be spotting similarities and differences — so the skills you practised in the last section will come in handy.

Warm-Up Activity

1. Find another person to play this game with you. <u>Cut</u> a piece of <u>card</u> into <u>18 squares</u>.

2. Draw each of these shapes on a different square: a <u>large red triangle</u>, a <u>large blue triangle</u>, a <u>large yellow triangle</u>, a <u>small red triangle</u>, a <u>small blue triangle</u>, a <u>small yellow triangle</u>. On the next 12 squares, do the <u>same</u>, but with <u>circles</u> and then <u>rectangles</u>.

3. <u>Shuffle</u> the squares and put them onto a table, <u>face down</u>. Take it in turns to turn over two squares. If they have <u>two things in common</u> (e.g. they're both small and red) you can <u>keep them</u>. If they don't, turn them back over and the other person takes their turn.

4. The <u>winner</u> is the person with the <u>most cards</u> when you can't make any more pairs.

The **Answer** has something **In Common** with the **Example Figures**

1) For these questions, you need to find something that <u>all</u> the example figures on the left of the page have <u>in common</u>, which <u>only one</u> of the answer options has too. That option is the <u>answer</u>.

2) In some sections you'll get <u>two example figures</u>, and in others you'll get <u>three</u>. You can use the <u>same method</u> to answer both types of question.

3) The answers might all <u>look quite different</u>. Remember that you're <u>not</u> trying to find the one that <u>looks</u> most like the examples — look for the <u>only one</u> with the right <u>elements in common</u> with them.

Sometimes you'll **Only** need to look at **One Element**

Look at the <u>most obvious</u> things first — they might give you the <u>answer</u>, or <u>narrow down</u> the options.

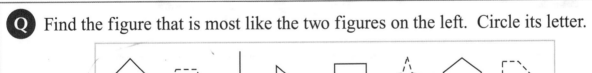

Q Find the figure that is most like the two figures on the left. Circle its letter.

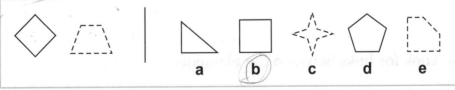

a b c d e

— Method 1 — Look for obvious similarities —

1) Find <u>one thing</u> that all of the example figures have in common.

2) If <u>only one</u> of the answer options also has that thing in common, then that must be the <u>answer</u>.

1) Both example figures are <u>white</u>, but all the options are also <u>white</u>, so that doesn't help. Each example figure has a <u>different type of line</u>, so that's not something they have <u>in common</u>.

2) Both example figures have <u>four sides</u>. <u>Only one</u> of the options has four sides — the answer is <u>B</u>.

Question Types — Similarities and Differences

You might need to look at **A Few** elements **Separately**

Often the example figures will have a few elements in common, that may not be linked. Instead of looking for all the similarities at once, use the method below.

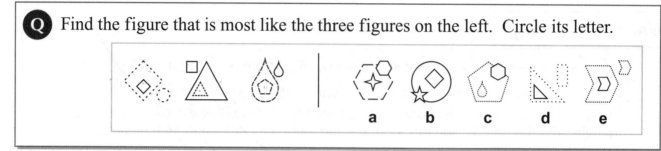

Q Find the figure that is most like the three figures on the left. Circle its letter.

a   b   c   d   e

┌─ **Method 2 — Look at one element at a time** ───────────

1) Find something that the example figures have in common.

2) Rule out the answer options that don't have the same element.

3) Repeat these two steps until you're only left with one option — that's the answer.

Don't spend too long on this method, though — if you can't find the answer, go on to the next method.

1) Type of line — in each figure, the large shape has the same type of line as one of the small shapes. This rules out A (the big shape's line is different from both small shapes) and B (all of the shapes have the same type of line).

2) Small shapes — in each figure, only one of the small shapes must be the same as the big shape. This rules out E (all the shapes are the same) and C (they're all different). The answer is D.

The similarity could be a **Link** between **Two Elements**

If it's not obvious what the examples have in common, look at how different elements are related.

Q

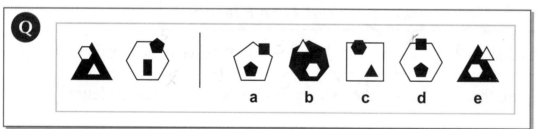

a   b   c   d   e

In this example, looking at the elements separately doesn't help you find the answer.

┌─ **Method 3 — Look for links between the elements** ───────────

Look at the different elements in the example figures to see if there are any links between them.

1) There aren't any links between the number of sides of the large shape and the two small shapes.

2) You could add up the number of sides of the two small shapes, but that doesn't help — the sides of the small shapes in both of the figures and all of the options add up to nine.

3) In the first example figure, the small shape at the top has six sides and the small shape below it has three. In the second figure, the small shape at the top has five sides and the small shape below it has four. The shape with the most sides is always on top.

4) Only option C has the shape with the most sides at the top — it must be the answer.

Question Types — Similarities and Differences

You *Might* need to *Look* for a *Pair* of *Rules* to find the *Answer*

1) For some questions, you might need to work out a <u>pair of rules</u>. The rules could be something like — 'If the shape is a square then it's white. If it's a circle then it's black'. The answer will be the <u>only option</u> which <u>follows</u> this rule.

2) <u>Only</u> look for <u>rules</u> if you <u>can't</u> solve the question any other way — rule questions are <u>very rare</u>.

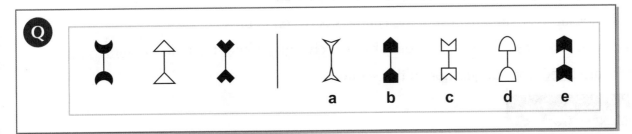

Method 4 — See if the example figures follow a pair of rules

1) Look for one example figure that has <u>two differences</u> from the other two example figures. In the middle example figure, the shapes at the end of the line are <u>white</u>, and have the <u>same rotation</u>, and in the others the shapes are black and are 180 degree rotations of each other.

2) Try to make a <u>pair of rules</u> out of these two differences. The rules in the example could be — 'If the shapes are <u>white</u>, then they have the <u>same rotation</u>. If they're <u>black</u> then they're <u>180 degree rotations</u> of each other.'

Odd One Out questions can have rules too, e.g. if the circle is inside the shape it's white and if it's outside it's black. The odd one out breaks the rule (the circle might be white and outside).

3) If <u>only one</u> of the answer options follows this pair of rules, then that's the <u>answer</u>. The <u>only answer option</u> to follow this rule is <u>D</u>, so this must be the answer.

Practice Questions

Which figure is most like the two figures on the left? Circle the right letter.

1)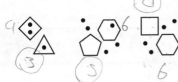

    a   b   c   d   e

Which figure is most like the three figures on the left? Circle the right letter.

2)

    a   b   c   d   e

3)

    a   b   c   d   e

Question Types — Similarities and Differences

Pairs, Series and Grids

These pages are about Complete the Pair, Complete the Series and Complete the Grid questions. Don't get your snap cards out yet, though — Complete the Pair isn't quite that fun...

You'll need to spot **How Figures Change**

1) These questions are all about spotting <u>changes</u> between figures.

2) Once you've spotted the change, you'll have to change <u>another</u> figure in the <u>same way</u>.

3) There are <u>three</u> types of question in this section:

Complete the Pair

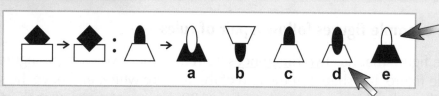

You've got to work out how the first figure changes to make the second. Then you need to make the same change to the third figure to find the answer.

The answer is D because the black shape moves from the back to the front.

Complete the Series

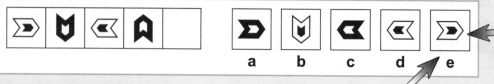

You've got to decide which of the figures on the right fills the gap in the series.

The answer is E because the arrow rotates 90 degrees clockwise in each square and the shading alternates.

Complete the Grid

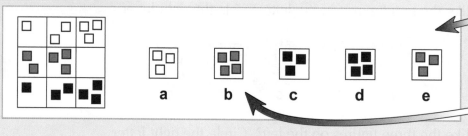

You've got to decide which of the figures on the right fills the gap in the grid.

The answer is B. The number of squares increases by one along each row, and all the squares in a row are the same colour.

Drawing the **Missing Figure** or **Writing Notes** can help you get started

These questions can be tricky at first, so here are some <u>tips</u> to help you <u>improve</u>.

1) Try <u>drawing</u> what you think should go in the <u>gap</u> in the series or grid, or what you think the <u>missing half</u> of the pair should look like. This'll help you to <u>imagine</u> what the answer should be.

2) You could also <u>write down</u> each <u>change</u> that you spot between the figures to <u>keep track</u> of them.

When you're more <u>confident</u> about these questions, and you're getting <u>close</u> to the <u>test</u>, you'll need to keep track of the changes and work out what the answer looks like <u>in your head</u>.

Complete the Pair

In these questions, you've got to be able to spot how one figure changes to make another one. There might be a few changes to notice, but don't worry — just look at them one at a time.

Warm-Up Activity

1. Find another person to play this game with. <u>Each of you</u> should <u>draw two boxes</u> on a piece of paper. Inside the <u>first box</u>, draw a <u>picture</u> (or a collection of shapes) and <u>colour</u> it in. In the <u>second box</u>, draw the <u>same picture</u>, but <u>change four things</u> about it.

2. <u>Swap</u> pictures, and take it in <u>turns</u> to spot the <u>four differences</u> between the two pictures and describe them to your partner. <u>Time</u> how long it takes each of you — the <u>winner</u> is whoever does it the <u>fastest</u>.

Work out how the **First** figure **Turns Into** the **Second** figure

1) For Complete the Pair questions you'll be given a <u>pair of figures</u>. You've got to work out which <u>element</u>, or <u>combination</u> of elements, changes in the first figure to <u>make</u> the <u>second</u> figure. Then you've got to change a <u>third</u> figure <u>in exactly the same way</u> to get the answer.

2) The first two figures might <u>look very different</u> from the third figure and the options. Remember that you're <u>not</u> looking for the option that's <u>most similar</u> to the first pair of shapes.

You might only need to spot **One Change**

In easier Complete the Pair questions, only <u>one thing</u> will <u>change</u> between the first and second figures.

Q Work out how the first shape is changed to make the second shape. Then choose the option on the right which goes with the third shape in the same way.

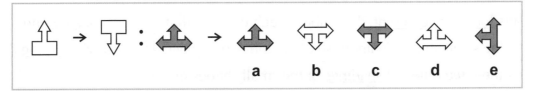

                                     a   b   c   d   e

Method 1 — Look at the elements that change

1) First work out <u>what happens</u> to the first figure to <u>make the second figure</u>.

2) Then <u>do the same thing</u> to the third figure to find the answer.

1) In this example, the first figure is <u>rotated 180 degrees</u> to give the second figure.

2) If you <u>rotate the third figure</u> 180 degrees you get the answer — <u>option C</u>.

For some questions you'll have to spot **More Than One Change**

For most Complete the Pair questions, <u>more than one thing</u> will change between each pair.

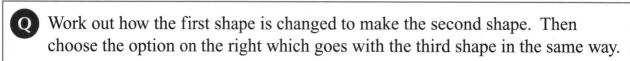

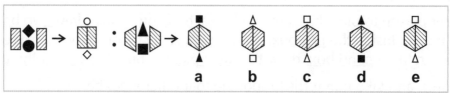

Method 2 — Narrow down the options

If <u>more than one thing</u> changes, use each change to <u>rule out</u> some possible answers.

1) <u>Small shapes</u> — the small shape at the <u>top</u> of the first figure moves to the <u>bottom</u> of the second figure, and the small shape at the bottom moves to the <u>top</u>. This means that the <u>answer</u> must have a <u>square</u> at the top and a <u>triangle</u> at the bottom. This <u>rules out</u> B and D.

2) <u>Shading</u> — the small shapes change from <u>black</u> to <u>white</u>. This <u>rules out A</u>.

3) <u>Hatching</u> — the hatching <u>rotates 90 degrees</u>. This means the <u>answer</u> must be <u>C</u>.

Sometimes the two pairs will look **Very Different**

The pairs <u>don't</u> have to look <u>similar</u> — sometimes they'll look <u>completely different</u>.
All that matters is that the <u>same change</u> happens between the two figures in each pair.

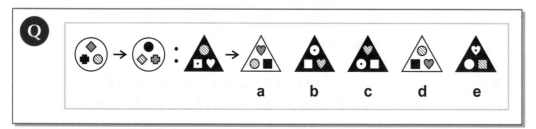

Even if the pairs <u>look</u> very <u>different</u>, think about each element that changes, <u>one by one</u>.

1) <u>Position</u> — the <u>small shapes</u> (without shading) move one place anticlockwise, <u>ruling out</u> B and D

2) <u>Shading</u> — the three different <u>shadings</u> of the small shapes move
   one place clockwise around the group. The answer is <u>E</u>.

Tips and Tricks for Complete the Pair questions

It's easy to confuse this type of question with a 'Find the Figure Like the Others'
question (p.33-35). In this example, A and D are more similar to the first pair —
they're there to confuse you. Remember what type of question you're answering.

The two **Halves** of each pair might **Look** very **Different**

Sometimes there will be a <u>big change</u> between the <u>first figure</u> and the <u>second figure</u> of the pair.

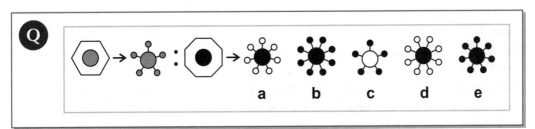

1) <u>Shading</u> — all the circles in the second figure have the <u>same shading</u> as the <u>circle</u> in the first figure. This means that the answer must have only <u>black circles</u>, which rules out A, C and D.

2) <u>Number of small circles</u> — in the second figure there are <u>five small circles</u>. This is <u>one less</u> than the <u>number of sides</u> that the white shape has. The white shape in the third figure has <u>eight</u> sides, so the answer must have <u>seven</u> small circles — the answer is <u>E</u>.

If the two figures in the first pair look very different, it's often a good idea to try counting things.

Tips and Tricks for the Test

If you're allowed to write on the test paper, put a line through the options you've ruled out. If you're not allowed, try putting one finger under every option, and then taking away your fingers as you rule them out. You'll end up pointing at the right answer.

Practice Questions

The first shape has been changed to make the second. Which option on the right relates to the third shape in the same way as the second relates to the first? Circle the right letter.

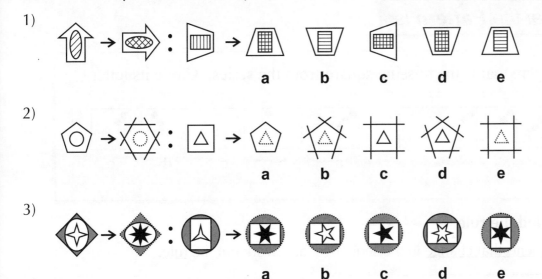

Complete the Series

For Complete the Series questions you've got to find the figure that completes a series. You'd never have guessed. These questions are all about sequences and patterns.

Warm-Up Activity

1. Find another person to play this game with you. <u>Each of you</u> should draw a <u>line</u> of <u>five boxes</u> on a piece of paper. Inside the boxes, draw a <u>sequence</u> of <u>pictures</u> of things that happen in <u>order</u> — it could be getting up in the morning, doing the washing up etc.

2. <u>Cut up</u> the lines of boxes, <u>shuffle</u> them and then <u>swap</u> them over. <u>Time</u> how long it takes to put the pictures back in the <u>right order</u>. The person with the <u>shortest time wins</u>.

You have to find the **Missing Figure** in a **Series**

In Complete the Series questions, you'll be given a set of <u>five figures in order</u>, with one figure <u>missing</u>. You've got to choose the option that <u>fills the gap</u>.

There are **Different Kinds** of **Series**

1) Things are <u>added</u> / <u>removed</u>:

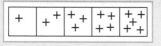

2) Things <u>alternate</u>:

3) Things <u>repeat</u>:

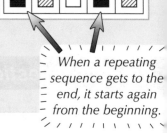

4) Things <u>move around</u>:

5) Things <u>change</u>, then <u>change back</u>:

When a repeating sequence gets to the end, it starts again from the beginning.

Work Out what the **Pattern** is

Q Find the figure that is the missing square from the series. Circle its letter.

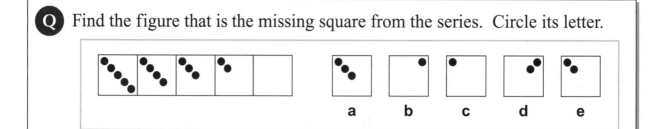

Method 1 — Find the rule

Look at any <u>elements that change</u> in the sequence, and work out the <u>rule</u>.

The <u>only element</u> that changes in this series is the <u>number of circles</u> — the bottom right hand circle is <u>taken away</u> in each series square. The circles that are left stay in the <u>same corner</u> of the series square. This means that the answer must be <u>C</u> because it has <u>one</u> circle in the <u>top left hand corner</u>.

Question Types — Pairs, Series and Grids

You'll normally have to find **More Than One Pattern**

Most questions have <u>more than one element</u> that changes. Each change could follow a <u>different rule</u>. Look at <u>each element separately</u> to see <u>if</u> it changes, and <u>how</u> it changes.

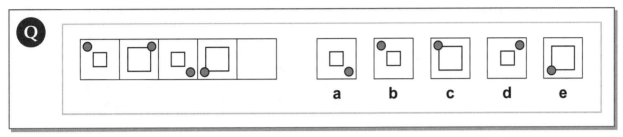

There are <u>two elements that change</u> in this series.

1) <u>Size of shape</u> — the size of the squares <u>alternates</u> between small and big.
   The fifth figure must have a <u>small square</u>, which rules out C and E.

2) <u>Position</u> — the circle <u>moves</u> around the <u>corners</u> of the series squares in a <u>clockwise</u> direction.
   This means that the fifth figure will have a circle in the <u>top left hand corner</u>, so the answer is <u>B</u>.

It **Won't Always** be the **Last Square** that's missing

1) <u>Any</u> of the five figures in the series could be <u>missing</u>. If the <u>first</u> figure is missing, you might have to work <u>backwards</u> from the <u>end</u> of the series to the <u>beginning</u> to find the answer.

2) If one of the <u>middle</u> figures is missing, look at the figures on <u>either side</u> of the missing square for clues.

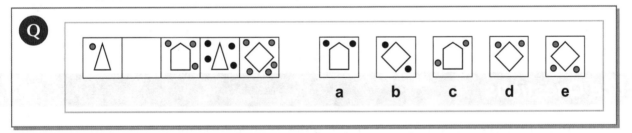

Method 2 — Look at the figures before and after the missing square

Look at each element that <u>changes</u> in the series:

1) <u>Shape</u> — counting the <u>number of sides</u> of the white shapes gives the sequence: 3, ?, 5, 3, 4. The sequence must be a <u>repeating sequence</u> which goes: 3,<u>4</u>,5,3,4,5 — the missing shape must have <u>4 sides</u>. This rules out A and C.

2) <u>Number of circles</u> — counting the <u>number of circles</u> gives the sequence: 1, ?, 3, 4, 5 — it <u>goes up by one</u> in each square. The missing square must have <u>two circles</u> — this rules out E.

3) <u>Colour of circles</u> — looking at the last three figures in the sequence tells you that the colour of the circles <u>alternates</u> between black and grey. The first figure has a <u>grey circle</u>, so the answer must have <u>black circles</u>. This rules out D, so the answer must be <u>B</u>.

Some sequences can look very **Complicated**

Harder Complete the Series questions will have <u>lots</u> of elements changing in <u>different ways</u>.

Q Find the figure that is the missing square from the series. Circle its letter.

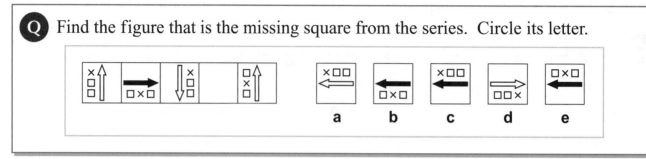

There are <u>four elements</u> that change in this series.

1) The <u>arrow rotates</u> 90 degrees clockwise — it must point <u>left</u> in the answer, which rules out D.

2) The <u>colour</u> of the arrow <u>alternates</u> between black and white.
The missing square must have a <u>black</u> arrow, which rules out A.

3) If each series square is <u>rotated</u> so the arrow points up, the squares and the cross <u>alternate</u> between being on the <u>left</u> and on the <u>right</u> of the arrow.
In the answer, they must be on the <u>right</u> of the arrow. This rules out B.

4) The <u>cross</u> moves one place <u>down</u> in each series square (if the series square is turned so that the arrow is pointing up). It must be at the <u>top</u> in the answer — the answer is <u>C</u>.

You need to look at the fifth square to work out that the cross goes: top, middle, bottom, top, middle, not: top, middle, bottom, middle, top.

Tips and Tricks for Complete the Series questions

Hard Complete the Series questions aren't really different from easier ones — they just have more things going on. Work out one rule at a time and rule out options as you go.

Practice Questions

Find the figure that is the missing square from the series. Circle its letter.

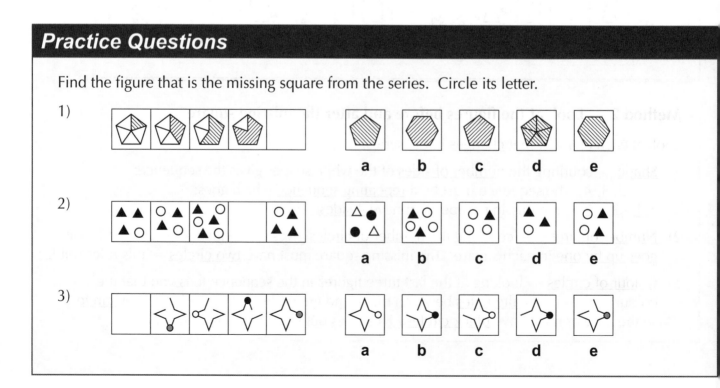

Complete the Grid

So the bad news is you've still got one more question type to get your head around in this section. The good news is that it's time for Complete the Grid, and everyone loves a grid.

Warm-Up Activity

1. Find another person to play this game with you. <u>Each draw</u> a <u>grid three squares high</u> and <u>three squares wide</u> on a piece of paper. Draw a <u>picture</u> that <u>fills all</u> the <u>squares</u> of the grid.

2. <u>Cut up</u> the grid, <u>pick one</u> of the squares and keep it <u>separate</u> from the others.

3. Try to <u>rearrange</u> the <u>other person's squares</u> to make the <u>original picture</u> (with a gap where the missing square should go). When you've made the picture, <u>draw what you think</u> should <u>go</u> in the <u>missing square</u> on another piece of paper.

4. The <u>winner</u> is the person whose <u>drawing</u> is <u>closest</u> to what's on the <u>missing square</u>.

You have to find the **Missing Figure** in a **Grid**

1) For Complete the Grid questions, you'll get a grid with either <u>four</u> or <u>nine</u> squares.

2) <u>Any one</u> of the squares might be <u>missing</u>, and you've got to find the figure that <u>fills it</u>.

3) Grid questions can work along <u>rows</u> (from left to right), <u>columns</u> (from top to bottom) or <u>both</u>.

Start by looking at **What Changes** across a **Row**

Rows go from side to side.
Columns go up and down.

The first thing you should do is look along a <u>complete row</u> to see what happens to <u>each element</u>.

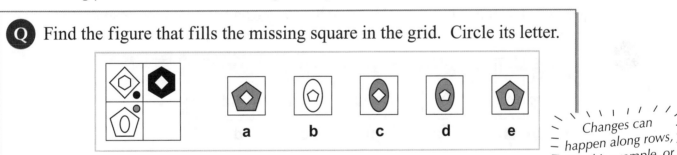

Q Find the figure that fills the missing square in the grid. Circle its letter.

    a   b   c   d   e

Changes can happen along rows, like this example, or down columns, like the first example on the next page.

Method 1 — Find out what changes along each row

1) Look at a row with <u>no gaps</u> and work out <u>what elements change</u>.

2) To find the missing grid square, make the <u>same changes</u> to the row with the gap.

1) In this example, moving from <u>left to right</u> along the top row, the <u>large</u> shape (diamond) gets <u>smaller</u> and the <u>small</u> shape (hexagon) gets <u>larger</u>. The large shape in the <u>right hand square</u> turns the <u>same colour</u> as the <u>circle</u> in the first square (the circle <u>disappears</u> in the second square).

2) To find the <u>missing square</u>, make the <u>same changes</u> to the bottom row of the grid. The <u>ellipse</u> gets <u>bigger</u> and the <u>pentagon</u> gets <u>smaller</u>. This rules out A, C and E. The ellipse turns <u>grey</u> (the colour of the circle). This rules out B, so the answer is <u>D</u>.

Question Types — Pairs, Series and Grids

Figures might be **Reflected**, **Rotated** or **Both**

This example works <u>down the columns</u>, instead of <u>across the rows</u>. You can work out what goes in the missing grid square in exactly the <u>same way</u> — just spot what's <u>changed</u> in the column without the gap.

Q Find the figure that fills the missing square in the grid. Circle its letter.

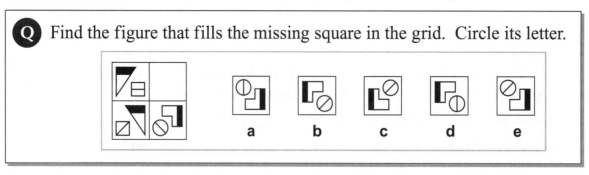

1) In the example, it's difficult to see any <u>connection</u> between the figures along each <u>row</u> — the shapes are very <u>different</u>. To find the answer, you need to look down the <u>columns</u> — the shapes in each column are <u>more similar</u> than in each row.

2) Looking down the <u>left hand column</u> (the one <u>without a gap</u>), the whole figure is <u>reflected across</u>. The <u>line</u> inside the square <u>rotates</u> 45 degrees anticlockwise going <u>down</u> the column.

3) The missing square is at the <u>top</u> of the grid, so you'll need move <u>up</u> the <u>right hand column</u> to find the answer — you'll have to make the changes <u>backwards</u>.

4) The bottom right hand grid square must be <u>reflected across</u> to make the top right hand grid square. The <u>line</u> inside the circle <u>rotates</u> 45 degrees clockwise (because you're moving <u>up</u> the column instead of down it). The answer is <u>D</u>.

Grids can work **Horizontally** and **Vertically** at the **Same Time**

In some questions looking at <u>just</u> the columns or the rows <u>won't</u> give you the answer.

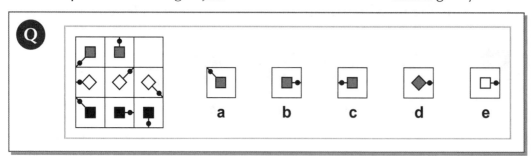

— **Method 2 — Look at the rows and the columns** —

Look at the <u>rows first</u>, and <u>rule out</u> as many options as you can. Then look at the <u>columns</u>.

1) In each <u>row</u>, all three small squares are <u>coloured</u> and <u>rotated</u> the same. This rules out D and E, but you're still left with <u>three possible answers</u>.

2) Going <u>down</u> each column, the black dot and the line rotate <u>45 degrees clockwise</u> around the grid square.

Treat each row and column as a 3-part series — spot patterns just like you would in a Complete the Series question.

3) The missing square is at the <u>top</u> of a column, so you've got to <u>work backwards</u> to find the answer — moving <u>anticlockwise</u> from the grid square below, the black dot must be in the middle on the right. The answer is <u>B</u>.

Question Types — Pairs, Series and Grids

The **Figures** in the **Grid** might make a **Pattern**

There are a few <u>different types</u> of pattern you need to look out for.

Different Kinds of Pattern

1) Two figures <u>alternate</u>.

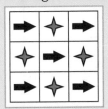

2) Each row <u>moves along</u>.

Each row moves to the left and a new figure is added.

3) The grid makes a <u>big picture</u>.

4) Each figure <u>only appears once</u> in each <u>row</u>, once in each <u>column</u>, or once in each row <u>and</u> column.

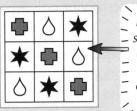

In this example, it's the shape that is different in each row and column, but it might be any element (e.g. line type, number or rotation).

5) Two different elements each <u>appear only once</u> in each row and column.

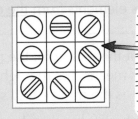

In this example, each number of straight lines (one, two and three) and each rotation of the lines both only appear once in each row and column.

Grids often have **More Than One Pattern** or **Sequence** to look for

The patterns above might be <u>combined</u> with other patterns or sequences.

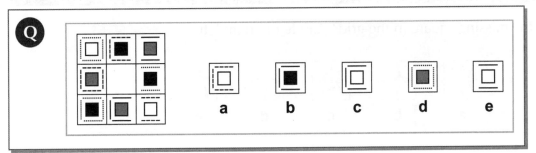

1) In this example, along the <u>top and bottom rows</u> (from left to right) the <u>number of lines</u> changes from <u>four</u>, to <u>three</u> and then to <u>two</u>. The missing grid square is in the <u>middle</u> of a row, so it must have <u>three lines</u>. This rules out D and E.

When the middle grid square of a row or column is missing, you'll have to look at the grid squares around it to find the answer.

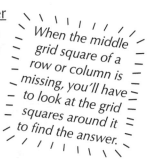

2) Each <u>shading</u> of square (black, grey and white) <u>only appears once</u> in each <u>row and column</u>. This means the answer must be <u>white</u>. This rules out B.

3) Each <u>type of line</u> (solid, dashed and dotted) <u>only appears once</u> in each <u>row</u>. This means the answer must have <u>solid lines</u>. This rules out A, so the answer must be <u>C</u>.

Two *grid squares might be* ***Added Together*** *to make the third*

Some questions don't have any pattern or sequence at all. Instead, the contents of two of the grid squares are added together to make the third one.

Q Find the figure that fills the missing square in the grid. Circle its letter.

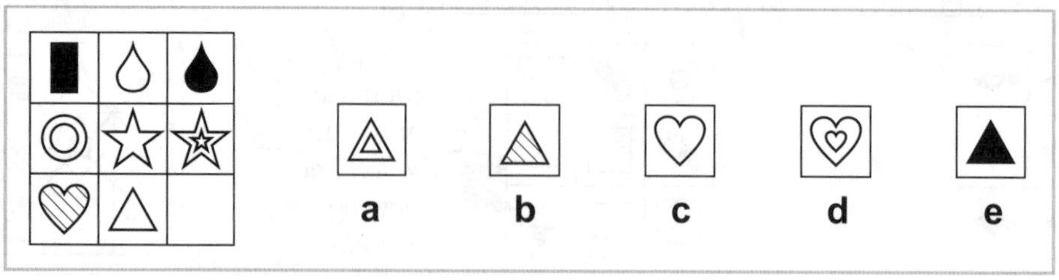

Method 3 — Look for figures that share elements with other figures

If you can't see a sequence or pattern in the grid, check the complete rows and columns for one figure that has elements from the other two figures in the same row or column.

1) In the top two rows of this example, the middle and right hand grid squares both have the same shape. This means that the right hand grid square in the bottom row must have the same shape as the middle grid square — a triangle. This rules out C and D.
2) In the top two rows, the left hand and right hand grid squares both have the same shading, so the missing grid square must have the same shading as the bottom left hand grid square — it must be hatched. This rules out A and E, so the answer is B.
3) For this example, the rule is that the figure in the right hand grid square in each row has the same shape as the middle grid square, and the same shading as the left hand grid square.

Practice Questions

Which figure fills the missing square in the grid? Circle the right letter.

1)

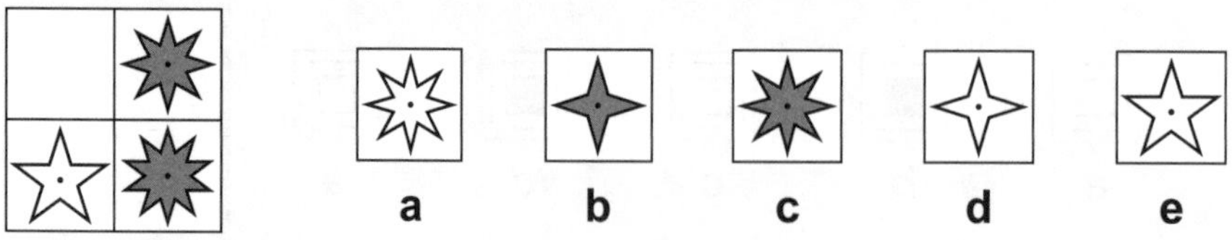

2)

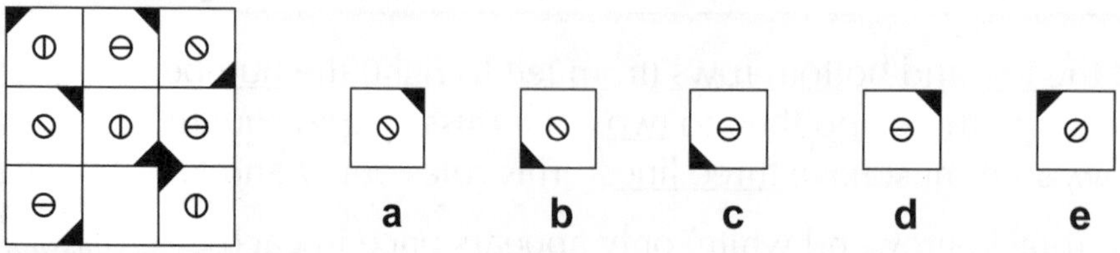

3)

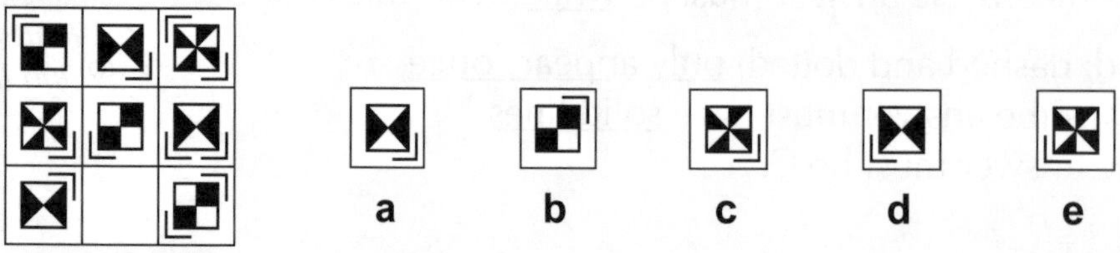

Codes

Luckily, the codes you'll have to work out aren't anywhere near as complicated as the codes that spies have to work out in the movies — at most you'll have to figure out three letters.

You'll need to **Crack** a **Code**

1) In code questions, you'll be given three or four figures with <u>code letters</u> that <u>describe</u> them.

2) You need to work out what each code letter <u>means</u> and then find the code for <u>another figure</u>.

3) There are <u>two</u> types of question in this section:

Vertical Code

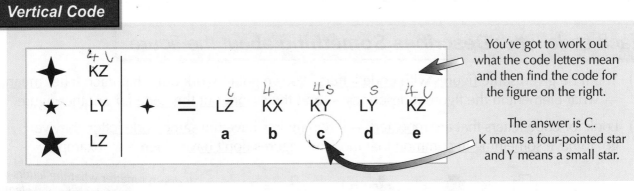

You've got to work out what the code letters mean and then find the code for the figure on the right.

The answer is C. K means a four-pointed star and Y means a small star.

Horizontal Code

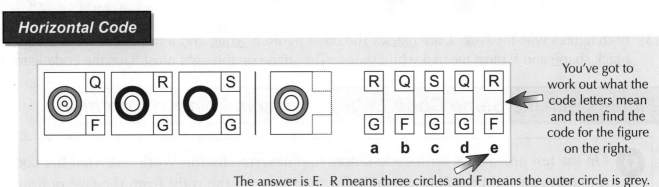

You've got to work out what the code letters mean and then find the code for the figure on the right.

The answer is E. R means three circles and F means the outer circle is grey.

Here are some **Tips** for **Starting Out** with **Code** questions

You probably won't be a codes expert <u>straight away</u>, so here are some <u>tips</u> to help you <u>improve</u>.

1) When you see a question for the first time, <u>circle</u> any repeated letters in the codes for the example figures. They'll be your <u>starting point</u>, so it's good to spot them straight away.

2) When you <u>work out</u> what one of the code letters means, <u>write it down</u>, e.g. B = three dots, C = two dots. This will help you <u>keep track</u> of what each letter means, and will make it <u>easier</u> to find the code for the figure on the right. It'll also help you <u>check your answer</u> if you get a question <u>wrong</u>.

3) As you find each <u>code letter</u> for the figure on the right, <u>write it down</u> so you don't <u>forget</u> it.

These tips are great for helping you <u>get the hang</u> of solving code questions, but in the <u>real test</u>, you won't have <u>time</u> to do all this. It'll still be useful to <u>write down</u> the code letters as you find them, though.

Vertical Code

Code questions can seem scary and complicated at first, but thankfully there's only one main method you need to know to solve them all. These pages will show you how to use this method.

Warm-Up Activity

On squared paper, draw the outline of a shape with straight lines. Each line must be one, two, three or four squares long. Write a code to show how to draw it using this key: A = 2 squares, B = 4 squares, C = 1 square, D = 3 squares. W = up, X = down, Y = left, Z = right. For example, CY = 1 square left. Give your code to a friend to see if they can use it to draw your picture.

Each code letter **Describes Something** about the figure

1) You'll be given some figures with code letters. You've got to work out what each letter means — what element in the figure it describes — and then work out the code for another figure.

2) Look for code letters that are repeated — if two figures have the same code letter, they've got to have something in common that the other figures don't have. Here's an example:

$$\boxplus = K \qquad \blacksquare = L \qquad \blacksquare = L \qquad \bigm| \qquad \boxplus = ?$$

It doesn't matter what the letters are — any letter can describe any element.

3) Both figures with the letter L are black. The other figure is white and it has a K. L must mean a black shape and K must mean a white shape. The shape on the right must have the code letter K.

Figures with the **Same Code Letter** have something **In Common**

Q On the left are shapes with code letters that describe them. Work out what the code letters mean and then find the code for the shape on the right from the five options.

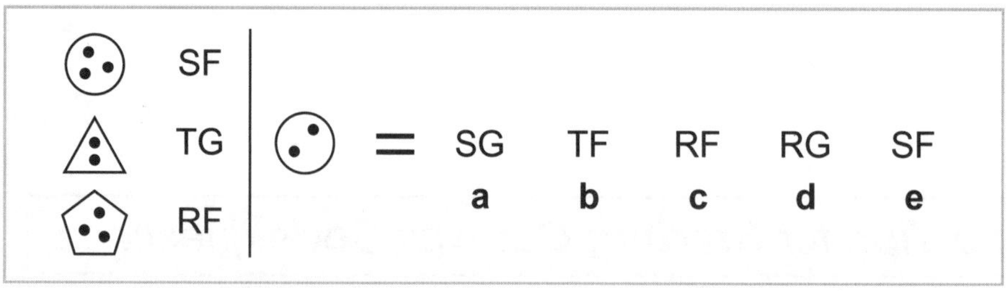

3 dots

⊙ (3 dots circle)	SF						
△ (triangle)	TG	⊙ =	SG	TF	RF	RG	SF
⬠ (pentagon)	RF		a	b	c	d	e

Method 1 — Look for repeated code letters

1) In the example, the first and third figures both have three dots and the letter F. The second figure has two dots and a G instead. The second code letter must stand for the number of dots — F means three and G means two. The shape on the right has two dots, so it has a G.

2) Look for code letters that don't repeat — they must stand for an element that's different in all the figures. In the example, the first letter in each code (R, S and T) aren't repeated. The only element that is different in each figure is the white shape. S means a circle, T means a triangle and R means a pentagon. The shape on the right is a circle, so its first code letter must be S. The answer is A — SG.

Some codes are **Trickier** than they **First Seem**

Always make sure the code works for <u>all</u> the figures — sometimes they're designed to be <u>confusing</u>.

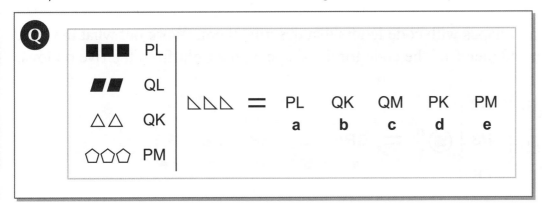

1) In this example, the <u>first</u> code letter is the easiest to work out — the figures with the <u>letter P</u> have <u>three shapes</u> and the figures with the <u>letter Q</u> have <u>two</u> <u>shapes</u>. The figure on the right has three shapes, so its first letter must be <u>P</u>.

2) The first and second figures are <u>black</u> and have the letter <u>L</u>. The second letter can't be for <u>shading</u>, though, because the other figures are <u>both white</u> and they have <u>different letters</u>.

3) Look at the first two figures again to see what else they have <u>in common</u>. Their shapes all have <u>four sides</u>. The shapes in the <u>third</u> figure have <u>three sides</u>, and in the <u>fourth</u> figure they have <u>five</u> <u>sides</u>. The second letter in the code stands for the <u>number of sides</u> the shapes have. The figure on the right has shapes with three sides, so its letter is <u>K</u>. The code is <u>PK</u> and the answer is <u>D</u>.

Vertical Code questions can have **Three Code Letters**

You can solve <u>three-letter</u> codes using <u>exactly the same method</u> as you did for <u>two-letter</u> codes.

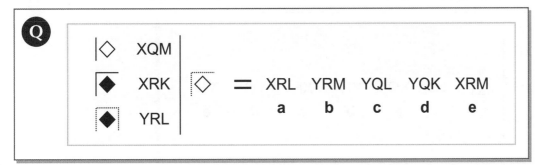

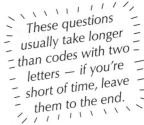

These questions usually take longer than codes with two letters — if you're short of time, leave them to the end.

1) The figures with the <u>letter X</u> have <u>solid lines</u>, and the figure with the <u>letter Y</u> has <u>dotted lines</u>. The figure on the right has a dotted line, so its first letter must be <u>Y</u>.

2) The second and third figures both have the <u>letter R</u>, and both have <u>black diamonds</u>. The first figure has a <u>white diamond</u> and the code letter Q. The figure on the right has a white diamond, so its second letter must be a <u>Q</u>.

3) The third letter is <u>different</u> for each figure, which means it stands for something that is <u>different</u> in all of them. The <u>number of lines</u> is the only thing that's different for each figure, so <u>M</u> must stand for <u>one line</u>, <u>K</u> for <u>two lines</u> and <u>L</u> for <u>three lines</u>. The figure on the right has two lines, so its final letter must be <u>K</u>. The code is <u>YQK</u> and the answer is <u>D</u>.

Not Everything in the Figure will be Part of the Code

Some elements aren't <u>included</u> in the <u>code</u> — none of the <u>code letters</u> describe them.

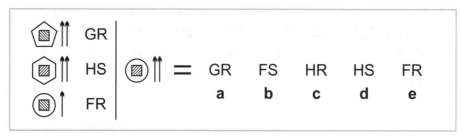

Q On the left are shapes with code letters that describe them. Work out what the code letters mean and then find the code for the shape on the right from the five options.

1) The <u>first</u> and <u>third</u> figures both have an <u>R</u>. The only thing they have <u>in common</u> (that's also different in the second figure) is the <u>direction of the hatching</u> in the small square. The figure on the <u>right</u> must have an <u>S</u> because its hatching matches the <u>second</u> figure.

2) The <u>first</u> code letter is <u>different</u> in all three figures. The only thing that's <u>different</u> in all three figures is the <u>white shape</u>. The figure on the <u>right</u> has the same white shape as the <u>third figure</u> (a circle), so its first letter is <u>F</u>. The answer is <u>B</u> — <u>FS</u>.

3) The <u>number of arrows</u> is the same in the <u>first two figures</u>, but they <u>don't</u> have any letters in common. The arrows <u>don't affect the code</u> at all — you can just <u>ignore</u> them.

Code letters can describe Combinations of Elements

Some code letters describe the <u>relationship</u> between <u>different elements</u> (e.g. the <u>number</u> of <u>lines</u> is the same as the <u>number</u> of <u>sides</u>, or two shapes are the <u>same colour</u>).

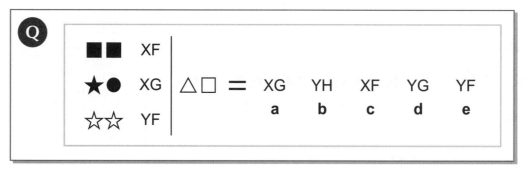

— **Method 2 — Look at different combinations of elements** —

1) The <u>first two</u> figures both have two black shapes and the letter <u>X</u>. In the third figure the two shapes are <u>white</u>, and it has the letter <u>Y</u> instead. The first code letter must stand for the type of shading. The two shapes in the figure on the right are <u>white</u>, so it has a <u>Y</u>.

2) The first and third figures both have an <u>F</u>. The only thing they have in common that's also different in the second figure is that both their shapes are the <u>same</u>. The second figure has two <u>different</u> shapes (a star and a circle), so <u>G</u> stands for having <u>different shapes</u>. The figure on the right has different shapes (a triangle and a square), so its second letter must be <u>G</u>.

3) The code must be <u>YG</u>, so the answer is <u>D</u>.

The *Most Obvious* answer *Won't* always be an *Option*

Sometimes you might think you've cracked the code, but then the figure on the right <u>doesn't fit</u>. If this happens, <u>don't worry</u> — just have <u>another look</u> to see if the figures have <u>anything else</u> in common.

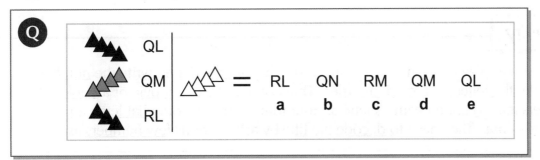

This example <u>looks simpler</u> than it actually is.

1) The first letter is straightforward — <u>Q</u> is for <u>four shapes</u> and <u>R</u> is for <u>three shapes</u>.

2) The most obvious meaning for the second letter is <u>colour</u> — <u>L</u> means <u>black shapes</u> and <u>M</u> means <u>grey shapes</u>. Watch out, though, because the figure on the right has <u>white shapes</u> and there's <u>no code letter</u> for white shapes.

3) <u>Have another look</u> at the figures on the left — the <u>first</u> and <u>third</u> figures both have the code letter <u>L</u> and are arranged going <u>diagonally down to the right</u>. The second figure has an <u>M</u> and is arranged going <u>diagonally down to the left</u>. The second code letter must stand for arrangement. The figure on the right is arranged going diagonally down to the <u>left</u>, so it must have an <u>M</u>, and the answer is <u>D</u> (<u>QM</u>).

You might think the answer is QN, and that N means white shapes. However, the answer won't contain any letters that aren't already on the left hand side of the question.

4) Don't worry if the code in the <u>answer</u> is the <u>same</u> as the code for one of the <u>figures on the left</u> — this sometimes happens.

Practice Questions

Find the code for the shape on the right from the five options. Circle the right letter.

1)

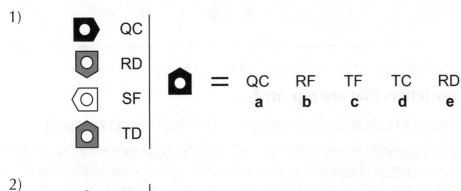

2)

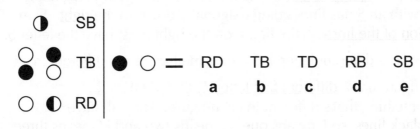

Horizontal Code

If you're not a fan of Vertical Codes, the bad news is that Horizontal Codes are pretty similar — they just look different. The good news is that you can solve them in exactly the same way.

Warm-Up Activity

Find another person to play this game with you. Write the alphabet, then write the numbers from 1 to 26 under the letters in a random order. Think of the title of a movie or a book but only write the numbers that go underneath its letters. Your friend can ask you what letter a number stands for, one at a time. They have to decode the title by asking for as few numbers as possible.

Horizontal Codes are like Vertical Codes

For Horizontal Code questions, you're given some figures with matching codes, and you've got to work out the code for a new figure — just like Vertical Code questions. They look a bit different though — here's the same question twice, first as a Vertical Code and then as a Horizontal Code.

> **Q** On the left are figures with code letters that describe them. Work out what the code letters mean and then find the code for the shape on the right from the five options.
>
>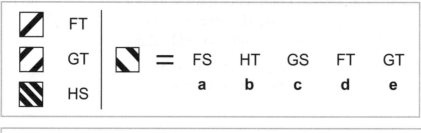
>
>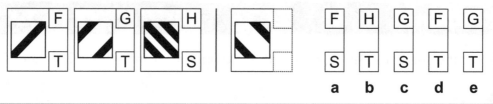

You can solve Horizontal Code questions in the same way as Vertical Code questions:

Method 1 — Start with any letters that are repeated

1) Look at two figures that share a code letter and find something they have in common.

2) In the example, the first and second figures both have a T and the only thing they have in common that the third figure doesn't have is that they have lines going diagonally down to the left. The figure with an S has lines going diagonally down to the right. S and T must be for the direction of the lines — the figure on the right must have the letter S.

3) If each example figure has a different letter, look for something that's different in each one.

4) In this example, each figure has a different first letter (F, G and H) so you should look for something that's different in each figure. They all have different numbers of black lines, so F means one, G means two and H means three. The figure on the right has two, so it must have a G. The answer is C (GS).

Make sure you don't **Mix Up** the **Letters**

It can be confusing if the letters on the <u>top row</u> describe the elements at the <u>bottom</u> of each figure, and the letters on the <u>bottom row</u> describe the elements at the <u>top</u>.

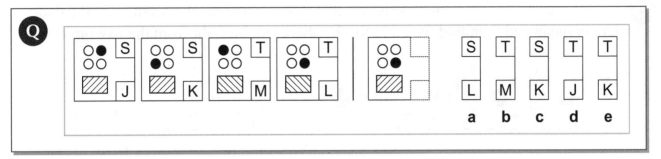

In this example, it's easy to <u>confuse</u> the <u>top</u> and <u>bottom</u> letters.

1) <u>Top letters</u> — the <u>first two</u> figures both have an <u>S</u> at the top. In both figures, the <u>direction of the hatching</u> inside the rectangle at the <u>bottom</u> of the figure is the same. The <u>second two</u> figures have the <u>opposite</u> direction of hatching, and they both have a <u>T</u> at the top. The figure on the <u>right</u> has the same direction of hatching as the <u>first</u> two figures, so it must have an <u>S</u>.

2) <u>Bottom letters</u> — the <u>bottom</u> letters are <u>different</u> in every figure. The <u>black circles</u> are in <u>different positions</u> in each figure, so the <u>bottom</u> letters must describe the black circle's position. In the figure on the <u>right</u>, the black circle is in the <u>same</u> position as the <u>fourth</u> figure, so it must also have an <u>L</u> at the bottom. The code is <u>SL</u>, so the answer must be <u>A</u>.

Sometimes you'll have to **Look Closely** to find the **Important Detail**

You might not be able to see the answer <u>straight away</u> — look <u>carefully</u> at all the details.

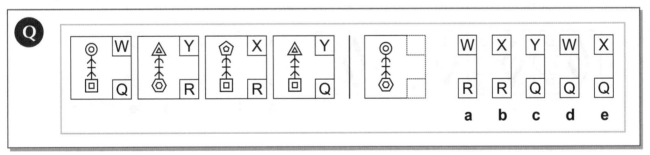

In this example, the answer isn't very <u>obvious</u>:

1) <u>Top letters</u> — the <u>second</u> and <u>fourth</u> figures both have a <u>Y</u>, and they both have a <u>triangle</u> on top. The other two figures have <u>different letters</u> (W and X) and <u>different shapes</u> (circle and pentagon). The <u>top letter</u> means the <u>top shape</u>. The figure on the right has a <u>circle</u> at the top, so its top code letter is <u>W</u>.

2) <u>Bottom letters</u> — both figures with <u>Q</u> have a <u>square</u> at the bottom, but one of the figures with an <u>R</u> also has a square, so Q and R <u>can't</u> mean the <u>bottom shape</u>.

3) The figures with Q have <u>two arrowheads</u> on the line — the figures with R have <u>one arrowhead</u> and <u>one semicircle</u>. The figure on the right has <u>one arrowhead</u> and <u>one semicircle</u> so it must have an <u>R</u>. The code is <u>WR</u> and the answer is <u>A</u>.

If you get really stuck solving one of the letters, pick an option that fits the letter you've worked out, and move on.

The **Right Code** might be one you've **Already Seen**

Sometimes the <u>code</u> for the figure on the <u>right</u> will be <u>the same</u> as for one of the figures on the <u>left</u>.

Q On the left are figures with code letters that describe them. Work out what the code letters mean and then find the code for the shape on the right from the five options.

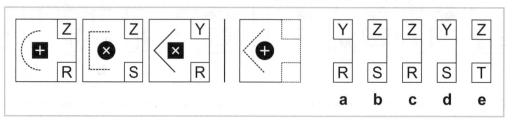

1) <u>Top letters</u> — in this example, the <u>first two figures</u> have the top letter <u>Z</u> and they both have <u>dashed lines</u>. The <u>third</u> figure has a <u>solid line</u> and the top letter <u>Y</u>. Z means <u>dashed lines</u> and Y means <u>solid lines</u>. The figure on the right has <u>dashed lines</u>, so it has the <u>letter Z</u>.

2) <u>Bottom letters</u> — the <u>first</u> and <u>third</u> figures both have an <u>R</u> on the bottom and they both have <u>black squares</u>. The <u>second</u> figure has a <u>black circle</u> and the letter <u>S</u> on the bottom. R means a black <u>square</u> and S means a black <u>circle</u>. The figure on the right has a <u>black circle</u>, so it has the letter S. The code for the figure on the right is <u>ZS</u>, so the answer is <u>B</u>.

3) This code is the <u>same</u> as the code for the <u>second figure</u>, even though they <u>look</u> quite <u>different</u>. The <u>rotation</u> of the <u>cross</u> and the <u>shape</u> of the <u>line</u> don't affect the code.

Practice Questions

Find the code for the shape on the right from the five options. Circle the right letter.

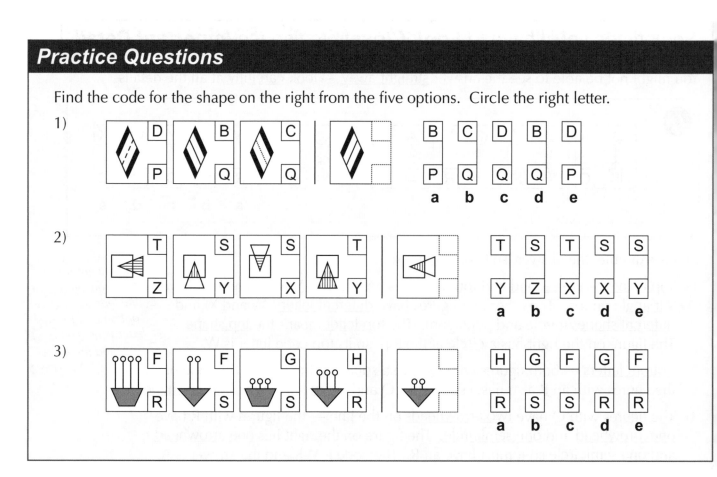

Answers

SPOTTING PATTERNS

PAGE 7 — SHAPES

Practice Questions

1.   D

All the other shapes have five sides.

(Counting the sides of each of the shapes shows you that D is the only shape that has a different number of sides from the rest, with four sides instead of five.)

2.   E

All figures must be triangles.

(Counting the sides of the example figures shows you that they both have three sides. E is the only figure that also has three sides.)

3.   E

The shape in the next series square always has one less side than the shape in the series square before it.

(Counting the sides of each of the shapes shows you that the number of sides of the shapes goes in the order: seven, six, five, four. This means that the next shape must have three sides. E is the only three-sided shape.)

PAGE 9 — COUNTING

Practice Questions

1.   B

All the other figures have the same number of lines crossing the outline of the shape as the number of black dots inside the shape.

(Keeping track of the number of small lines and dots in each figure shows you that there is a connection between the two types of object. B is the only figure which does not share this connection — it has two lines and three dots.)

2.   A

All figures must have three less black shapes than the number of sides of the outer shape.

(Counting the number of sides of the large shape and the number of black shapes in the example figures shows you that there is a connection between the two — the first example has six sides and three black shapes, the second example has five sides and two black shapes. A is the only figure which has three less black shapes than the number of sides of the large shape, with four sides and one black shape.)

3.   A

The large shape gains an extra side in each series square. An extra black dot turns grey in each series square.

(Keeping track of the number of sides, black dots and grey dots in each figure shows you how many sides and dots the next figure should have. The number of sides goes in the order: three, four, five, six. The next figure must have seven sides. The number of grey dots goes in the order: one, two, three, four. The next figure must have five grey dots. The number of black dots goes in the order: five, four, three, two. The next figure must have one black dot. A is the only figure which has a seven-sided shape, five grey dots and one black dot.)

PAGE 11 — POINTING

Practice Questions

1.   D

In all other figures the arrow is pointing away from a four-sided shape and towards a circle.

(If the arrows in all the figures don't share a common direction you should check whether the arrows all point towards or away from a common shape. D is the only figure in which the arrow points towards a four-sided shape and away from a circle.)

2.   E

The arrow switches between going clockwise and anticlockwise. The length of the arrow decreases in each series square.

(You can see that the arrow gets shorter in each square, so you don't have to work out how much smaller it is getting to realise that the missing square must have the smallest arrow. This means you are left with a choice between C and E. The arrow swaps between going clockwise and anticlockwise, and the arrow in the fourth square is going anticlockwise, so you know that the arrow in the missing square must be going clockwise. This leaves you with E as the answer.)

3.   E

All arrowheads must point right.

(By looking at the example figures, you can see that they both point in the same direction. E is the only figure which also points right.)

PAGE 14 — SHADING AND LINE TYPES

1.   E

All shapes must be hatched and have a dashed outline.

(Looking at the example figures, you can see that they are both hatched. This leaves you with a choice between A, D and E. The two example figures also have the same sort of dashed outline. A has a solid outline, and D has a dotted outline, which leaves you with E as the answer.)

2.   D

An extra two squares turn black in each series square.

(The number of black squares goes in the order: two, four, six, eight. The missing figure must have ten black squares. D is the only figure with ten black squares, so it must be the answer. You could also work out the answer by looking at the white squares, which go in the order: fourteen, twelve, ten, eight. The missing figure must have six white squares, which also gives you D.)

3.   E

All the other figures are made up of four lines.

(By counting the lines for each figure you can see that E has five lines, while the rest only have four. You could also look at the number of gaps in each figure's outline to work out the answer.)

56

PAGE 17 — POSITION

Warm-Up Activity
Tangram Square

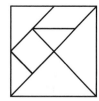

Practice Questions

1.   D

The heart moves round the shape one side at a time in an anticlockwise direction. The arrow moves up the middle of the hexagon, until it gets to the top, and then it starts moving down the middle of the hexagon.

(By working out the movement of both the small shapes, you know that the next square must have the arrow at the bottom of the hexagon, and the heart on the right hand side of the hexagon. D is the only option that fits both of these descriptions.)

2.   C

In all other figures, the shapes are in the same positions — in C the circle and the raindrop have swapped places.

(Checking the position of each shape in turn will help you spot any differences.)

3.   C

In each series square, a shape is removed in a clockwise direction.

(Counting the shapes in each square shows you that there is one less shape each time, going in the order: six, five, four, three. The missing figure must have two shapes. This leaves you with a choice between C and E. Because the shapes are removed in a clockwise direction the triangle should be the next shape to disappear. In E the star has been removed, which leaves you with C as the answer.)

PAGE 19 — ORDER

Practice Questions

1.   D

Working clockwise, the shapes in all the other figures go in the order: ellipse, star, triangle, trapezium.

(Picking the same small shape on the outline as a starting point and then counting round in the same direction for each of the figures will help you work out if the shapes are in an order. The order is the same for all the figures, apart from D, which has the order: ellipse, trapezium, triangle, star.)

2.   E

All the shapes move one place to the left in each series square.

(The shapes in all the examples have the same order: triangle, circle, square, hexagon (going from left to right). When the shape on the left hand side can't move any further left, it appears again on the right hand side in the next series square. E is the only figure where all the shapes are in the right order and the right positions: triangle, circle, square, hexagon (from left to right). Because there are only four shapes and four positions, it looks identical to the figure in the first square.)

PAGE 22 — ROTATION

Practice Questions

1.   D

All the other figures are identical apart from rotation.

(If you turn the page so that all the shapes are rotated the same as figure C, you can see that D is a different shape. D has the thinner horizontal bar at the top of the shape and the thicker horizontal bar at the bottom of the shape. In all other figures, the thinner horizontal bar is at the bottom, and the thicker horizontal bar is at the top.)

2.   B

The black quarter circle rotates 45 degrees anticlockwise around the centre of each series square. The diamond rotates 90 degrees anticlockwise in each series square.

(To help you see the rotation of the quarter circle, pick one of the straight edges of the quarter circle and see how it has rotated in the next square. The quarter circle in the missing square must be a 45 degree anticlockwise rotation of the quarter circle in the fourth square, so it must be in the bottom left of the square. This leaves you with a choice between B and E. Picking either the grey or the white half of the diamond and following it round will help work out how the diamond is rotating. The next square must have the diamond rotated so that the grey half is at the top, which leaves you with B as the answer.)

3.   C

Ignoring the hatching, the right hand shape in all figures must be a 90 degree clockwise rotation of the left hand shape. The hatching in the right hand shape must be a 45 degrees anticlockwise rotation of the hatching in the left hand shape.

(This question shows why you should always double check how the hatching of a shape changes. If you thought that both the shape and the hatching rotated 90 degrees together, you would get D as the answer. If you work out the rotation of the right hand shape, you are left with a choice of C, D and E. C is the only option that has the correct hatching rotation. Rotating the page might help you work out how the shape and hatching should look in the right hand shape.)

PAGE 25 — REFLECTION

Practice Questions

1.   B

In all other figures the bottom shape is a downwards reflection of the top shape.

(Imagining a horizontal line dividing each of the figures in half might make the reflection easier to see. The black shading of the bottom shape in figure B is the wrong way round for it to be a reflection — the bottom shape is actually a 180 degree rotation of the top shape.)

2.   E

In all figures the right hand shape must be a reflection of the left hand shape across the dashed line.

(Looking at the first two figures, they both have a dashed line going diagonally down to the left. The left hand shapes are reflected across this line to become the right hand shapes. It might help you see the reflections better if you turn the page so that the line is horizontal. E is the only option where the right hand shape is a diagonal reflection of the left hand shape.)

Answers

3.   A

The shape rotates 90 degrees anticlockwise round the middle of each series square. After rotation, the shape reflects back on itself over its longest side.

(This is quite a difficult question because the mirror line changes position in each square. To make it easier to see the mirror line you could rotate the page so that the shape is always at the bottom of each square.)

PAGE 28 — LAYERING

Practice Questions

1.   E

In all other figures, the hatched shape is a 90 degree clockwise rotation of the shape made by the overlap of the two white shapes.

(The hatched shape in figure E is not the same shape as the overlap of the two white shapes, no matter how it is rotated — it's actually the shape left when you take the overlap away from the triangle.)

2.   B

All figures must have a black shape at the front, and a white shape at the back.

(Looking at the example figures, they both have shapes layered in the same order from front to back: black, grey, white. A has both the white shape and the black shape at the front. C and D both have the grey shape at the front. E has a grey shape at the back, which means that B is the only option that has the colours on the right layers.)

3.   C

Working from front to back, all other figures go in the order: pentagon, ellipse, hexagon, arrow.

(You can check the order by picking the same shape to start with in all figures, and counting from that shape back. In C, the arrow and the hexagon have swapped places, giving the order: pentagon, ellipse, arrow, hexagon.)

QUESTION TYPES

PAGE 32 — ODD ONE OUT

Practice Questions

1.   B

All of the other figures have a solid outline.

(The figures are all the same colour and all the shapes are different, so neither of these things help you find the odd one out. A, C and D are symmetrical, but B and E don't have any lines of symmetry, so symmetry doesn't help you either. They all have solid outlines except B which has a dashed outline, so this must be the answer.)

2.   D

In all other figures, the ends of the curved lines point away from the ellipse. In D, they point towards the ellipse.

(All five of the figures are identical except for rotation, colour and the direction the curved lines point in. Figures A, C and D have the same colour scheme as each other. Figures B and E have the same colour scheme as each other, so colour doesn't help you find the odd one out. Figures A, B and D are rotated the same way, and figures C and E are rotated the other way, so rotation doesn't help you either. Only D has its curved lines pointing in a different direction from the other four, so that must be the odd one out.)

3.   A

In all other figures, two of the arcs have their gaps facing the black dot, and one has its gap facing the edge of the hexagon.

(All the figures are white hexagons with black dots in the centre, and they all have three arcs, so none of these things are helpful when you're looking for the odd one out. In figures A, B and D there's one arc at the top and two at the bottom. In figures C and E, there are two at the top and one at the bottom — this doesn't help you find the odd one out either. Only A has arcs pointing in a different direction to the rest, so this must be the answer.)

PAGE 35 — FIND THE FIGURE LIKE THE OTHERS

Practice Questions

1.   C

All figures must have a small white shape inside a larger grey shape.

(The example figures both have two shapes, and one of the shapes is inside the other one. This leaves options B and C. In both the example shapes the inside shape is white. Figure B has a grey inside shape, which means the answer must be C.)

2.   D

In all figures, the number of black dots must be the same as the number of sides on the shape with the smallest number of sides.

(The first example figure has three dots, one shape with three sides and one with four sides. The second example figure has five dots, one shape with five sides, and one with six sides. The third has four dots, one shape with four sides, and one with six sides. D is the only option that shares the same connection as the example figures, with four dots, one shape with four sides, and one with five sides.)

3. B

In all figures, the arrow must go clockwise around the circle. The beginning and the end of the arrow must line up with the beginning and the end of the black segment of the circle.

(In all three of the example figures, the arrow goes clockwise around the circle. Figures C, D and E have arrows going anticlockwise. This leaves options A and B, so you've got to look back at the example figures to see what else they've got in common. In all the example figures the arrow lines up with the beginning and end of the black segment of the circle. The arrow in figure A doesn't line up with the black segment of the circle. This means that B is the answer.)

PAGE 39 — COMPLETE THE PAIR

Practice Questions

1. D

The figure is rotated 90 degrees clockwise and the hatching becomes crosshatched.

(In the first pair, the ellipse and the arrow both rotate 90 degrees clockwise together. The hatching inside the ellipse changes from being hatched to crosshatched. The same thing must happen to the second pair — the rectangle and the trapezium rotate 90 degrees clockwise together, so that the shortest side of the trapezium is at the bottom. This rules out A, C and E. The hatching inside the rectangle becomes crosshatched. This rules out B, so the answer is D.)

2. B

The large shape gets an extra side, and the lines that form its sides get longer so they cross each other. The outline of the small shape changes from solid to dotted.

(In the first pair the pentagon gains an extra side, so it becomes a hexagon. The lines that make up the hexagon's sides get longer so they cross over. The inner shape's outline changes from solid to dotted. This means that the square in the second pair gains an extra side so it becomes a pentagon. This rules out C and E. The lines that make up its sides get longer so this rules out A. The small triangle's outline changes from solid to dotted which rules out D, so the answer is B.)

3. A

The larger white shape rotates 90 degrees and the outline of the grey shape changes from solid to dotted. The number of points on the star doubles and it turns black.

(In the first pair, the ellipse rotates 90 degrees. The outline of the diamond changes from solid to dotted. The star turns black, and gains four points to become eight-pointed (it could be doubled or four points could be added). In the second pair the rectangle rotates 90 degrees, which rules out E. The outline of the grey circle changes from solid to dotted, which rules out D. The star turns black which rules out B. Adding four points to the star gives you seven points, but there aren't any options like this, so the number of points must be doubled to six points. This rules out C, which means the answer must be A.)

PAGE 42 — COMPLETE THE SERIES

Practice Questions

1. A

In each series square, another section of the pentagon becomes hatched in a clockwise direction. The line between the old hatched section and the new hatched section disappears. The hatching rotates 90 degrees in each series square.

(Each large shape in the series is a pentagon, which rules out B and E. The lines between the sections disappear when the sections become hatched, which rules out D. The hatching from the fourth square rotates 90 degrees, which rules out C, so the answer must be A.)

2. E

The number of black triangles alternates between three and two. The number of white circles changes in the pattern: one, two, three, two, one.

(All of the series squares have black triangles and white circles — this rules out A. Looking at the squares on either side of the missing square shows you what the sequence should be. The number of triangles changes in the sequence: 3, 2, 3, ?, 3. The missing square must have two black triangles, which rules out C. The number of circles changes in the sequence: 1, 2, 3, ?, 1. It could either go: 1, 2, 3, 4, 1, or: 1, 2, 3, 2, 1. None of the options have four white circles, so the sequence must be: 1, 2, 3, 2, 1 — so there must be two white circles. This rules out B and D, so the answer must be E.)

3. B

In each series square, the circle moves clockwise around the four points of the star. The gap in the star's outline moves one side clockwise. The colour of the circle changes in the order: black, grey, white, black, grey.

(Working backwards along the series (from right to left) you can see the circle and the gap in the star's outline moving anticlockwise around the star. The next position the circle will be in is on the right hand point of the star (this doesn't rule out any options). The next position the gap will be in is on the top of the star's left hand point. This rules out A, D and E. If you follow the pattern of the colour of the circle backwards along the series, you know that is has to be black (it's a repeating three-colour sequence) which rules out C. B must be the answer.)

PAGE 46 — COMPLETE THE GRID

Practice Questions

1. D

Working from left to right, the number of points on the star doubles and it changes colour from white to grey.

(Since the missing grid square is on the left, you should reverse the change to move from right to left — the star changes colour from grey to white, so the answer must be white. This leaves options A, D and E. The number of points on the star goes down by five, but you can't tell whether the points are removed, or whether they've been halved (both methods would give you five points). If five points were removed, the star in the answer should have three points. None of the options have three-pointed stars, so it must be halved. The star must have four points, which leaves you with D as the answer.)

2. B

Working from left to right, the black triangle moves one place clockwise around the four corners of the grid square. Each rotation of the line in the circle (vertical, horizontal and diagonally down to the right) only appears once in each row and column.

(To find the missing grid square, move the black triangle from the bottom left hand grid square one corner clockwise. It will be in the bottom left hand corner of the grid square, which leaves options B and C. Then work out which rotation of circle hasn't appeared in the bottom row and the middle column — the answer must have a line going diagonally down to the right. This rules out C, so the answer must be B.)

3. E

Each shading inside the squares only appears once in each row and column. Along each row, the grid square on the right contains both of the right-angled lines from the left hand grid square and the middle grid square.

(The only shading which hasn't already appeared in the bottom row and the middle column is the shading made of eight triangles, which leaves options C and E. Looking along the first two rows, the right hand grid square has two right-angled lines and the other two squares only have one. The two in the right hand square are in the same positions as the two in the left hand and middle squares. On the bottom row, the two lines are in the top right and bottom left hand corners. The left hand square has a right-angled line in the top right, so the answer must have one in the bottom left hand corner. This rules out option C, so the answer must be E.)

PAGE 51 — VERTICAL CODE

Practice Questions

1. D (TC)

Q = pentagon pointing to the right, R = pentagon pointing down, S = pentagon pointing left, <u>T</u> = pentagon pointing up. <u>C</u> = black pentagon, D = grey, F = white.

(Both of the figures with grey pentagons have the letter D in common, and the figures with C and F each have different colours. The second letter must describe the pentagon's colour. The right hand pentagon is black, so it must have a C. The first letters are all different and the only thing that's different in all the figures is the direction the pentagon points in. The first letter must describe the pentagon's direction. The right hand pentagon is pointing up, so it must have a T.)

2. D (RB)

<u>R</u> = two circles, S = one circle, T = four circles. <u>B</u> = half of the figure is black, D = a quarter of the figure is black.

(The first and second figures have the letter B in common, and both figures are half black. The figure with a D is only a quarter black, so the second letters describe how much of the figure is black (you could also work this out by looking at how much of each figure is white). The right hand figure is half black so it must have a B. The first letters are all different and the figures all have a different number of circles. The first letter must describe the number of circles. The right hand figure has two circles, so it must have an R.)

PAGE 54 — HORIZONTAL CODE

Practice Questions

1. A (BP)

<u>B</u> = the line in the middle of the diamond is solid, C = the line is dotted, D = the line is dashed. <u>P</u> = the lines go diagonally down to the left, Q = the lines go diagonally down to the right.

(The second and third figures have the letter Q in common and they both have lines going diagonally down to the right. The figure with P has lines that go diagonally down to the left. The bottom letters describe the direction of the lines. The right hand figure has lines going diagonally down to the left, so it must have a P. The letters in the top line are all different, and the only thing that's different in all figures is the type of line in the middle of the diamond. The top letter must mean the type of line. The right hand shape has a solid line, so it must have a B.)

2. B (SZ)

<u>S</u> = only the tip of the triangle is hatched, T = the whole triangle is hatched. X = the triangle is above the square, Y = the triangle is below the square, <u>Z</u> = the triangle is to the right of the square.

(Both of the figures with a letter S have the tip of the triangle hatched, and both of the figures with a letter T have the whole triangle hatched. The top letters describe how much of the triangle is hatched. The right hand figure only has the tip hatched, so it must have an S. Both of the figures with a letter Y have the triangle underneath the square, and the figures with X and Z both have the triangle in different places. The bottom letter must describe the position of the triangle. The right hand figure has the triangle on the right, so it must have a Z. The direction of the hatching doesn't matter.)

3. B (GS)

F = long lines between the circles and the grey shape, <u>G</u> = short lines, H = medium length lines. R = the number of circles (and the number of lines) is the same as the number of sides of the grey shape, <u>S</u> = the number of circles is one less than the number of sides of the grey shape.

(Both of the figures with long lines have the letter F. The other two figures have different letters and their lines are different lengths, so the top letter must describe the length of lines. The right hand shape has short lines, so it must have a G. The first and fourth figures both have the letter R. In the first figure, the grey shape is four-sided and there are four circles. In the fourth figure, the grey shape is three-sided and there are three circles. The second and third figures both have the letter S. In the second figure, the grey shape is three-sided and there are two circles. In the third figure, the grey shape is four-sided and there are three circles. Comparing these numbers shows you that the bottom letters describe how many circles there are compared to the number of sides of the grey shape. The right hand figure has a three-sided grey shape and two circles, so it must have an S.)

Answers

Index